con verg ence

Technology, Business, and the Human-Centric Future

Deborah Westphal

Foreword by **Beth Comstock**

Former Vice Chair of G.E.

un

ISBN: 978-1-951213-24-4
EISBN: 978-1-951213-26-8

Library of Congress Control Number: 2021933960

This book is a work of nonfiction.

Cover design by Robert Bieselin
Typeset by Jaya Nicely

Manufactured in the United States of America by Sheridan Books.

Distributed by Publishers Group West

First Edition

For Gregory and Michael

table of contents

con
verg
ence

foreword

I'm a big believer in future-focused thinking. Deb Westphal is too.

One of the greatest challenges of our time is that too many businesses think only of today. I worry that our traditional business schools limit their teaching to what's certain and provable. They offer great tools to assess business and build strategy while neglecting to teach a systematic approach for thinking about the future.

Maybe that's why, if you look across most industries, you see a discomfort with the concept of emergent leadership. Many leaders neglect or delegate the hard work of planning for the future. I get it. It can seem like guesswork. Our time horizons continue to shorten, so everything seems urgent. The future is coming at us fast and from every direction. Change is happening at the points where technologies, people, and things are converging.

When I wrote *Imagine It Forward*, I realized how helpful it would have been in my early career at General Electric to have understood how critical it is to think about the future. Over time, I learned that lesson through hard feedback.

What I learned is that good leadership is not just about knowing and executing business processes. It's about seeing around corners, asking good questions, challenging old knowledge, and being open to sharing ideas and vision. As Deb shows us throughout this book, with those things in mind, we can find great leaders everywhere. She makes a powerful case for why change is everyone's job and shows that leaders aren't out creating the future so much as they are approaching it with humility and inspiring others.

We know that tomorrow always comes. We have to build resilience in our organizations by doing the work to survive to see tomorrow. There isn't the time to decide *if* we're going to look or imagine forward. We simply must, and quickly and constantly.

In the stories, examples, and observations throughout this book, Deb offers practical ways to recognize where to create change and what doing so means for your organization. We have to make time for trendspotting and looking out for what may seem weird. That's where growth and possibility live.

I love that every chapter begins with a quote from Alvin Toffler, one of the foremost futurists of our time. He also was Deb's mentor. Those quotes and the relationship she had with the Tofflers give even more reason to listen to the guidance she shares. It's easy to fall into thinking that the future is opaque and the idea of convergence is complex. But in an approachable, systematic way, Deb shows that convergence is fundamentally the idea of "and": business *and* politics; technology *and* humanity.

Think about technology and humans for a second. People are adaptive champions because of our humanity. We developed technology to help us evolve, and in a short measure of time, we've gotten perilously close to losing sight of where our responsibility ends and technology begins. As we converge deeper with technology, we risk forgetting that it works for us, not we for it.

The balancing act between humanity and technology is just one example of why convergence may seem complex. But if we remember that leadership is about people working with people to solve problems, it becomes simpler to identify what technology can and can't do for us. This idea is a through line in *Convergence*.

The first two chapters lay a perfect foundation for understanding the confluence of technology and humanity. Deb launches the book with a chapter called "Knowing Humans." In it, she shows that technology is the tool and people are the energy source. Without humans, technology is rudderless. That human-centric approach becomes the groundwork for understanding and navigating change. Chapter 2, "The Human System," provides a systematic structure for making decisions that satisfies the needs of both people inside the organization and those served by it.

Throughout my career, I've seen how helpful these careful practices and habits are to leaders and their companies. It recognizes our need to connect with and listen to other people as we deal with uncertainty and decision-making. By focusing on people, we are reminded that useful knowledge resides everywhere.

Sometimes people get so embedded in their corporate position that they begin to believe they can't learn anymore. It's not true. Knowledge is distributed. Once we accept that fact, we can spot what we know and then open ourselves up to what we don't. By exposing ourselves to the unknown and clearing out ideas and information that have become obsolete over time, we position ourselves to look forward and make confident decisions.

This is the future of leadership (and leadership for the future).

A human-centric, technology-enabled leadership approach might seem different from how we've been trained. It might seem soft. But it's vital. We can't lose sight of the fact that we're all humans, working together in a system that is impacted by our environment, technologies, and other things. In that regard, convergence is about being more of what we already are.

I find that comforting. As leaders, we're looked to for answers. Deb points out that the leaders who can take people through change are ones who recognize they don't know everything. That not everything is answerable. And that we're moving forward with a hypothesis until new information asks us to think differently.

Even if the pathway isn't well defined—*especially* if the pathway isn't well defined—we have the power to navigate change and build resilience by recognizing that we can create and use convergences to our advantage. Occasional failure is likely. That's okay. Throughout the book, you'll find a solid, approachable framework for being future focused. Take a moment to skim the table of contents. When you do, you'll see the basic building blocks for developing human-centric change in your organization. Deb has provided a literal checklist of the things you need to do and a framework to get going. She's also a gifted storyteller. The examples that introduce each chapter provide models of real human behavior and frame the insights and knowledge that follow.

Through this groundbreaking book, Deb has emerged as a *translator* for the future. And she's generous enough to provide the encouragement, humanity, and systems approach necessary for you to build this leadership superpower.

We ignore tomorrow at our own peril. There's never been a time when it's more important to optimize for today and build for tomorrow. Especially for today's emerging leaders, *Convergence* is required reading.

—Beth Comstock
www.bethcomstock.info

introduction

We all face countless entirely new problems, challenges, and struggles, as a new economy and a new civilization arise on the planet—it is a fantastic moment to be alive. *Bienvenido al siglo veintiuno.*
—Alvin Toffler, 2001

Straddling the equator approximately a thousand kilometers west of Ecuador, you will find the Galápagos Islands archipelago. With 127 islands, islets, and rocks and roughly 133,000 square kilometers of protected ocean surrounding them, it is one of the largest marine reserves in the world. It enchants with incredibly clear aquamarine water and a mix of tropical and temperate climates. It was here in the 1830s that the famed naturalist Charles Darwin germinated the seeds of what would decades later become the theory of evolution by natural selection.

Galápagos may be one of the most fascinating and unique places on Earth. The islands are famous for their wide range of endemic species of plants and animals. But it is their distinct set of environmental conditions that set them apart from all other island groups in the world.

The Galápagos archipelago formed as perpetually moving pieces of Earth's crust caused volcanic eruptions at the bottom of the ocean. Even today, this area is one of the most volcanically active regions of the world. In fact, it is the only place in the world where six active volcanoes can be found within a small area roughly the size of Washington, D.C. Ongoing seismic and volcanic activity continue to shape and reshape the archipelago. More important than the volcanic activity, though, is the fact that the Galápagos Islands lie at the convergence of three major ocean currents. It is the cross flow of these currents that stimulate the islands' unique ecology.

The Humboldt Current is massive, sweeping north up the western edge of South America, carrying cold, nutrient-rich water from Antarctica along the coasts of Chile and Peru. At the equator, the Humboldt joins the westward South Equatorial Current and the warm, southward-flowing Panama Current before heading straight toward the Galápagos. About three hundred feet below these three surface currents is the Pacific Equatorial Undercurrent. An immense river within the ocean, it is one of the most vigorous currents in the world. It extends about one hundred miles wide and is the length of a football field deep. When it hits the Galápagos from the west, it deflects toward the surface, bringing cool, nutrient-rich water from the ocean floor to the archipelago.

The convergence of perpetual volcanic activity and ocean current movement is what makes the Galápagos the world's most productive ecosystem. And it is a fitting analogy to the convergences happening in today's business environment.

The islands that make up the Galápagos are like our businesses today. Some are small, some are large, and some are just emerging or reshaping as a result of seismic disruption. Some of the disruptions are minor, such as a small earthquake, and leave little trace of the event. Others may be major disruptions that can literally change the landscape. Neither of these types of changes is predictable; they just happen. But all reside and are shaped by an ecosystem created by swirling forces of change, which, much like the ocean currents, are the sources of life for today's business.

Let's think of the Humboldt Current as technology and the Pacific Equatorial Undercurrent as humanity in our analogy. Both are essential. In the Galápagos, the combination of the two currents sustains the richness of unique flora and fauna on the islands. In our contemporary business environment, both technology and humanity are vital. If one of these forces ceased to exist, became inordinately weak compared with the other, or changed direction, it would endanger the life of our businesses. That shift in the balance of technology and humanity is exactly what is happening in our current business ecosystem, and it threatens the companies we lead and the business climate in which we operate.

Now let's say that the third current, the Panama Current, represents our modern business structure and operating principles. As the immense wave of technology advancements have combined with contemporary business vectors, it has created divergences between *how* and *why* a business exists. In some cases, this third force has eradicated humanity's direction and energy, creating a fracture that threatens present-day business. More important, it threatens a sustainable business future. Overwhelmingly, the momentum of this growing divergence places business at high risk for hardships and, worse yet, failure.

To avoid the imminent and lasting detriment to our business climate brought on by the changing forces within it, we must rebalance the energy and focus we place on technology and humans. And as we do, we must readjust our thinking and subsequent actions about the purpose of business and the organization mechanisms we create to deliver on that purpose.

You may be thinking, *Easier said than done.*

Understanding how the changes outside the organization mandate the changes inside the organization is critical work. Deciding how and when our organizations must pivot to meet future challenges is taxing. It demands objectivity. But it also demands subjectivity, correctly applied. It takes honesty and courage to consider what's working and what isn't to create new behaviors and business practices to evolve and operate in a host of environments. It is essential to resilience.

Ultimately, the call to action must give preference to a human-centric perspective to meet head-on the momentum of further divergence. Momentum is hard to stop. To slow the velocity of something takes an equal or greater counter-force to push against it. The more momentum, the harder it is to slow down. And the pace of creation and adoption of technology by businesses is almost unprecedented. We won't slow or harness it successfully without focusing on cultivating an equally strong human-centric perspective for our organizations. It is at this intersection that we can seek an equitable convergence between the forces of technology, organization, and humanity that will set us up for equitable coexistence.

This is about how humanity is altering modern-day business. We are at an inflection point in history, a time that requires us to prioritize creating human-centric organizations to recalibrate how energy is spent on technology and people. Without such a reprioritization of effort, there is a substantial risk of creating a feedback loop that will result in the destruction of human life as we know it.

This book orients us to a rare and wondrous moment of massive disruption within a constant flow of change. It is a call to action for today's leaders to recognize the many signals of accelerating disruption. It is an encouragement to put away business practices, beliefs, and structures that no longer are pertinent or productive for surviving and thriving within an ongoing technological explosion that has no clear trajectory. And this book will often speak directly to *you*, as a business leader or future leader who has the ability to make critical changes to your fundamental business values. That said, this book was not written *just* for you. Rather, this book is for anyone with a stake or interest in the increasing convergence where people, technology, and business intersect. We *all* need to know what a human-centric organization looks like in order to know what to advocate for in the best interests of community, environment, and, indeed, our future.

The old "universal laws" of business are not universal any longer. As we transition further from industrial models of business that emphasize stability, order, uniformity, and equilibrium, those who excelled at managing these closed systems with linear relationships are increasingly feeling as if they are losing ground in the race to succeed. That is because they are.

Industrial society depended on heavy inputs of tangible assets, including land, nonrenewable resources, and capital. In today's business climate, information, innovation, and human energy have become critical resources. And as we move deeper into the Knowledge Age, intangible assets become more necessary. This shift demands new models. We face a reality characterized by inevitable social change: disorder, instability, diversity, disequilibrium, and nonlinear relationships. Small inputs from a few people can trigger massive consequences for our organizations, economies, or geopolitical relations; moments of change are only becoming more prevalent, networked, and extendable. Regardless of whether consequences are positive or negative, we must understand that business mechanisms have changed because everything is connected. People inside and outside your organization have the power to create these tipping points. As a result, we must change the way we do business.

A human-centric perspective sees customers, employees, suppliers, and communities not as entities to produce and serve *for* but rather to produce and serve *with*. This corporate purpose goes beyond maximizing shareholder profit. Being a human-centric enterprise means optimizing around people both inside and outside the organization instead of allowing process or structure to dictate decision-making and direction.

Human-centric is neither an end state nor a fixed design. It cannot necessarily be benchmarked against other organizations. It is uniquely its own, because it is cultivated by behaviors and mindsets that flow deeply within each specific organization. A human-centric organization embraces the messiness and beauty of people. Its policies and processes are highly iterative, rather than linear and standardized. It seeks to understand people and the effects of changing humanity so that it may continuously challenge and redefine business strategies and goals for both itself and the people it serves.

Tapping Into the Source

Organizations put so much energy into managing the organization and optimizing for return that the real power for innovation, creativity, and growth gets lost. Success requires human energy. Yet this incredible source of difference and growth is more often than not deprioritized through myopic views of the purpose of business and the models required to perform. Without a human-focused counterbalance, adopting advanced technology such as artificial intelligence, machine learning, and automation will continue to marginalize people, rather than centering them. Admittedly, this is a dystopic view straight out of science fiction. It is also increasingly a potential reality.

Today's organizational norms suck human energy from solving business challenges or meeting growth demands in a rapidly changing environment. For example, the constant focus on managing quarter by quarter financial numbers can drain innovation and risk-taking. And yet humans, both inside and outside the formal borders of an organization, are the central power source for business.

A pivot to a human-centric business practice requires re-organizing, beginning with seeing our customers, employees, suppliers, and communities not as entities to do *for* but rather to do *with*. Within organizations, we often try to label these people as "stakeholders," and yet we perceive them as little more than details on a checklist we must track and manage. They are not a corporate responsibility program or campaign that can be used by public relations professionals to support branding and goodwill. They are actual people with needs, hopes, desires, and fear for the future. They share the sense of citizenship that expects proactive, rather than reactive, behavior from the business.

The term *stakeholder* is overused. As a result, it's been robbed of meaning, becoming little more than jargon. It is often synonymous with *customer* or *user*. The broader, more accurate concept of the stakeholder is critical to the discussions throughout this book. We should use the term with care and precision to keep the human at the center. Instead of speaking in generalities, we should specify the person or group: customers, employees, suppliers, communities, or humanity at large.

It is no longer good enough to call these groups "stake-holders," because, while they have an interest or concern in your business, that title hardly encapsulates their importance to the purpose and performance of the organization. You must seek to partner with them to increase the impact and outcomes for them and for your business. In doing so, you establish a common purpose, a synchronization of needs.

In nature, when something stops growing and evolving, it dies. Yet we also know that change is guaranteed. And we know it is accelerating. It is complex. What we will not know is what the future will look like or its orders of impact. By replacing a business practice checklist that works well in the current context with a mental model that steadily considers human behavior and changing norms (for example), we can ask the right questions to assess what beliefs and methods are relevant, which are out of date, which create future risk, and which position everybody for success.

Going forward, you will need to build and maintain a broader understanding of the world around your business. You can no longer process knowledge through a belief system focused solely on increasing profits for those who benefit from them. Maintaining relevance and competitive positioning mean including considerations that may seem ancillary to today's core operations. It will likely take new voices from unexpected places to jolt us to look up, ask fresh questions, and think differently.

Where will you find these new voices? More important, will you be willing to listen and learn from these different perspectives?

The belief in human-centric change is the platform on which this book exists. Many of the ideas in *Convergence* reflect the future-focused approaches that Alvin and Heidi Toffler introduced so many years ago and that have only grown in importance since. While we work diligently to address the massive changes happening today, we must also keep an eye on the horizon for a much more radical transformation coming: a power shift fueled by human energy.

Convergence is a fact of life, society, and business. What you're about to discover is perspective, not prescription. In the chapters ahead, you'll learn from decades of innovation work in the public and private sector, timeless insights from the Tofflers, and the experiences of some of the most influential business, academic, and civic leaders of our age.

My hope for ambitious young professionals reading this book is that you find insights and information that resonate with your upbringing in the technology revolution. You are digital natives with perspectives that are unique and full of rich insight that is essential to our shared future. Your passionate and mission-driven approach to work and community is needed. Your commitment to affecting positive change in your organization and society is required. I hope you come away feeling that you are not alone in your pursuits. You are a member of a cohort of individuals who are open to new mental models and to doing things differently. I also hope it doesn't take you thirty years to figure out things like it did me. You don't have that much time. None of us do.

For those entrenched or traditional business leaders, I hope you come away motivated to lead urgent and necessary change. Your experiences and expertise are needed for making a vital shift within your organization, but radical change is required. Fifty years ago, the life expectancy of a Fortune 500 company was approximately seventy-five years. Now it is less than fifteen. This challenging, changing environment demands new ways of thinking about business and new mental models for leading effectively. I hope I challenge you to imagine and understand the future in a way that helps you shape decisions and actions today that position your organization for success tomorrow. I hope you learn something new that you can use to ensure your organization's relevance and resilience. I hope you embrace vulnerability and being uncomfortable, because personal growth is messy and, at times, scary.

Lastly, regardless of your age or position, I hope you gain an understanding of how core concepts developed by the Tofflers over five decades apply today to strategy and decision-making in contemporary organizations. These concepts are even more important now than they were when first introduced in their books.

Convergence continues the Tofflers' dedication to advocating for future consciousness. Alvin and Heidi Toffler truly believed in the empowerment of individuals to proactively create the future rather than being idly subjected to it. They spent a lifetime championing humanity. It is their legacy. It is what they passed on to me. And it is what I am honored to share with you.

Onward.

chapter one
Knowing Humans

> Out of this massive restructuring of power relationships, like the shifting and grinding of tectonic plates in advance of an earthquake, will come one of the rarest events in human history: a revolution in the very nature of power.
>
> —Alvin Toffler, *Powershift* (1990)

Meeting Angela Ahrendts was happenstance. It was 2015, and we were both attending Bloomberg's "The Year Ahead" CEO conference. She was a guest speaker. Sitting behind her, I noticed that as she waited for her turn at the speaker platform, she listened intently and took copious notes. Now and then, she would turn to share a thought or look of surprise with the person beside her. She was actively participating in the event, and she seemed to be having fun. When the time came for Ahrendts to speak, she stepped onto the low-rise platform, settled comfortably into a big fluffy chair, and joined in a casual discussion with the interviewer.

Apple CEO Tim Cook had recently talked Ahrendts into leaving her position as Burberry CEO to fill the role of senior vice president of retail at Apple. The interview session focused on her corporate transition. Ahrendts shared her fascinating story about crossing over from fashion to technology. Her key message centered on how important it was for business to be human-centric. She said that at Burberry, she encouraged the company to operate as a *business of people* that just happened to deliver on its promise through fashion retail. She planned to do the same thing at Apple: help the company understand people first, and then build and promote the technology business to follow.

Ahrendts was more than inspiring. She was authentic and real. As I sat in the audience, I felt a connection. Her beliefs seemed to come from her heart as well as her head.

At the end of her time, she wasn't swept away by her handlers as many speakers often seem to be; she simply returned to the chair she previously occupied and continued to take notes and share moments. At a break in the program, we both got up. I took the opportunity to introduce myself and let her know how much I appreciated her authenticity and the energy she seemed to have for people. We chatted for a few minutes about the importance of being empathetic and focused on people in today's business environment.

A few months later, I came across a 2013 video of Ahrendts giving a TEDx presentation in Hollywood. She offered a profound perspective on how human energy has the power to single-handedly unite people and transform companies and communities: "I believe we . . . all take in and we all emit energy. Very few leaders talk about it, and even fewer have mastered it. But when you find it, energy is like discovering your passion, listening to it, exploring it. It's like this forward-charging spirit that creates challenges and embraces . . . change in challenges."[1]

Her comment resonated because of its truth. Human energy is the ground state of our existence. It defines our humanness and all of humanity. It is the consciousness that allows us to self-organize and self-evolve. It connects our minds with our hearts to create that drive toward a purpose. While hard to describe, we feel it inside ourselves and recognize it in others. Instinctively we are drawn to it and seek to be a part of it.

Ahrendts challenged the audience to see human energy as emotional electricity with the power to create confidence and a sense of belonging. Leaders who can unite the people in their organization and harness their collective spirit can propel them to do and give more. They can create the fuel the organization needs to accomplish extraordinary things. Organizational progress would emerge from the shared perception, willingness to embrace ambiguity, and desire to work in unison toward a higher purpose for the organization. This, Ahrendts asserted, is what leaders do: they embrace humanity.

Power Shift

Many people say that we are in the midst of a tech revolution. They argue that technology is the supreme driving force for change in the world. Billions are spent advancing technology in an attempt to capitalize on this perception. However, at the core of the revolution, there's a human movement, one that reflects our need to connect, belong, and matter. No doubt, technology is changing the way we live, work, and engage with one another. But it is driven by our evolving expectations, hopes, dreams, fears, and desires. In this way, technology is adapting to our influence as much as we are influenced by it.

Technology may be pervasive and powerful, but it's social revolution that ultimately will have the greatest, most formative impact on our businesses. For today's leaders, this human revolution comes with an imperative. We must optimize value by fully taking advantage of people's uniqueness, both inside and outside our organizations. For businesses to succeed into the future, humanity must be a counterbalance to the technology that is increasingly taking hold of the world, connecting people within the organization and people outside it. That's a balancing act that can determine whether a movement becomes a threat or an opportunity.

As Ahrendts so aptly observed, "Technology is the conduit . . . [people] are the content. Or if technology is the physical connector, [people] are the emotional connector." We must understand how diverse human values and priorities create the energy and power that define organizational boundaries.

The reality is, with technology becoming more and more ubiquitous, people are becoming *more* important, not less. Only humans can bring the energy—the emotional electricity—that transforms companies, governments, and societies into forces capable of accomplishing extraordinary things. As we observed in the forces at work in the Galápagos Islands, the ecosystem survives through its balance of currents. In the same way, our organizations are not reliant solely on the impact of technology or humans—they require the confluence of both.

Evolutionary Momentum

We think about technology as applications, interfaces, and, most often, gadgets. That perception, while accurate, is profoundly limiting. Technology is perhaps the most concrete manifestation of human consciousness, evolving since the first stone chopping tool emerged nearly two million years ago. Categorically, it encompasses the entirety of human-made artifacts that have facilitated, and in some cases represented, human evolution.

Technology is a product of human action, and its role in society is well within our control. The prevailing thought used to be that, because technology was everywhere, it was the primary influence on society. Those beliefs and perspectives continue to evolve. Technology may influence us, but it is neither deterministic nor fated to be so. The choices we make as individuals, businesses, and societies determine how technology advances. As its intimacy with every aspect of human life grows more profound, these choices are more complex to be sure, and all the more important.

Nonetheless, technology is recombinant, so it grows as it's used and shared within and across networks. Growth and progress accelerate when technology is adopted, especially by large systems. Modern businesses may be the best examples of large systems that use technology to operate internally and influence externally, then extend their advancements across an even larger industry system. These *systems of systems* expand as complex, intertwined combinations of people, platforms, products, and services. The progress is exponential.

As technology successfully enhances outcomes in one part of the system, other parts are more likely to adopt it for themselves. Technological advancements are developed and introduced into these systems, impact happens, adoption increases, and the rate of change accelerates.

Technology is uniquely powerful and needy. It is an ever- expanding network of abilities and dependencies that continually redouble. This growth cycle is one reason we feel change accelerating to the point of sensing we might be on the verge of swerving out of control. Compared to the evolutionary pace of technology, humans seem to be falling behind. Of course, we are not. The relationship is symbiotic. The very technology upon which we're so reliant for connection and progress could not exist without humans.

The Strata from Human to Humanity

There's a hierarchy of human needs that builds from fundamental biological and psychological requirements to a higher level of motivation that encompasses self-esteem and self-actualization. The premise of this ladder of conditions is that only after people have satisfied their basic body-mind requirements can they attend to those that exist higher up. Put simply, we can achieve love and belonging only after we have secured our food, shelter, and safety.[2] Yet, as we consider the vitality of collective humanity and the power of human energy, we must acknowledge that love and belonging are very nearly as crucial and foundational to our survival as food and shelter.[3]

This argument does not undermine the consequence of our basic needs for safety, shelter, and food. It acknowledges that humans are social animals. We need attachments. We need to feel like we belong. Connection with others is a prerequisite for physical and emotional survival and is fundamental to our identity and place in the world. Those relationships mature and strengthen into collections—organizational constructs that become entities capable of producing their own energy, productivity, and outcomes. Belonging and connections are not just primary needs; they may very well be the driving forces of modern human evolution. They also may be the driving forces of the next-generation organization.

We grow as individuals only through intentionality. This is true for you, for me, and for everyone we know. We each dream about what to do with our lives. We set goals for ourselves and set out on paths to achieve them. Our experiences inform our cognitive processes of perception, memory, judgment, and rea-soning. We adjust our behaviors when obstacles get in the way of accomplishing the plans we create for ourselves. We enlist others—like mentors, peers, and other trusted partners—to help us along our journey. We learn from our mistakes. And we grow.

Collective intentionality also exists. Shared objectives transform conventions, norms, and group-minded beliefs and behaviors into complex organizational interactions. Together in groups of individuals, we set directions and processes, collaborate, coordinate actions, and share the tasks necessary to achieve common goals and outcomes. This ongoing process has created a broad spectrum of wonderful societies that coexist in modern life.

As societies become more complex, interconnected, and specialized, our reliance on one another grows. These vital human connections are nonlinear, meaning that they do not necessarily develop predictably. Instead, they progress in a random, multidirectional, and sometimes seemingly illogical fashion. Of course, we do act with intentionality to form connections. We might connect with someone on LinkedIn or ask someone to be a mentor. More often, however, relationships happen by chance as a result of factors like circumstance, proximity, belief systems, or timing.

As technology has given us the capacity to blow open these traditional relational boundaries, even humans who historically have had little power can become forces of opportunity, disruption, even existential threat to organizations and systems. The proliferation of social platforms and explosive growth in their use is proof of our instinct and desire to connect with others and to belong. People of every age, location, and standing seek these online environments to find their place in the world and act on motivations and goals in new and broader ways. The blistering rate of adoption should come as no surprise, considering that these technologies are our best means of securing and satisfying our basic survival instincts on levels from the most personal to the widest, most global.[4]

In the online world, as in the physical one, the ways we engage in social behavior map to the evolutionary shifts in humanity. Before social media, we gathered in community centers like church socials, Friday night bingo, and VFW halls to connect and stay informed about our relationship networks. As we glean more and more insights from the explosive use of social technologies like Zoom, Google

Hangouts, Snapchat, Facebook, and Twitter for work and social communication, we see just how vital social connection is to fulfilling our human needs, and how vital those technology platforms are to enabling them.

Still, it's dangerous to try to position social technology as more than what it truly is: a tool. True, it is a vital facilitator of human goals, but its power is limited to the extent of human intervention.

The unifying need for connection and belonging, and the pervasiveness of technological tools to enable it, should prompt a new question. Instead of asking, "What does technology do for us?" we must ask, "What can I do better with technology?" The answer is—and will continue to be in the future—that we should use current and emerging technologies to mobilize collective human energy for positive outcomes.

The New Global Community

As of the writing of this book in 2020, almost 60 percent of the world's population has access to the internet. More than four billion people actively use some form of social media.[5] This number is incredible, considering that only 68 percent of the world's population uses modernized sanitation facilities. The sheer scale and reach of communication networks have shifted the paradigm of citizen expression. New communication structures that lack hierarchy and boundaries are taking the place of traditionally gated ones, opening up previously untouchable spheres of power, influence, and association.

The growing capacity for people to communicate and collaborate over digital networks shows no signs of slowing. We are poised to take another giant leap in satellite communication constellations. A handful of companies, including SpaceX, Amazon, OneWeb, and Telesat, are racing to build and launch thousands of satellites to bring the internet to even the most remote and rural corners of the world, connecting "the other three billion" disadvantaged users.

Only twenty-five years ago, the idea of connecting eight billion people across the globe to one another via a "world wide web" provided by a fleet of communication constellations was little more than a pipe dream of entrepreneurs and space visionaries. Today, it is close to becoming a reality. The pace of advancement and adoption is blistering. Its impact on humankind is almost beyond measure.

Relevant manufacturing and launching processes like these satellite endeavors are opening doors to new, viable communication infrastructures. On May 30, 2020, more than ten million people tuned in on the internet to watch a SpaceX Falcon 9 rocket launch two men into space on the Crew Dragon Demo-2 mission to the International Space Station (ISS). The rocket stage that pushed Crew Dragon to the ISS returned safely to Earth, accomplishing an incredible feat that has opened the door to affordable space launch and a way for satellite communication companies to transport their constellations. The human impact of this progress is tremendous. It could mean affordable internet access for everyone, making that communication platform a truly global public commodity. And the corporate chain of impact is far from its end. Creative business models are emerging to amplify the access and usefulness of this critical communication infrastructure.

As technological innovation brings more people online, connects them, and gives them voice, we have seen a significant rise in online civil society activity. This wide-ranging array of organizations includes community groups, nongovernmental organizations, indigenous groups, charitable and faith-based organizations, and professional associations. With these platforms, bridges, and abilities to find (or create) a virtual community of similarly minded people, we are redefining the boundaries of civilization.[6] Today, all the people on the planet have approximately three degrees of separation from one another. Soon, that separation will be even smaller.

Modern civil society is a diverse and ever-widening eco-system of individuals, communities, and organizations. Our ability to more easily connect with others anywhere in the world, and to join our voices on issues and topics, is altering value systems and creating new societal norms. In just a few short decades, the web has made it quicker and easier to find people "like you"—others who share similar belief systems, experiences, affinities, and even DNA. With a few clicks of the keyboard, people across an organization, town, country, or planet can become part of your network. They may look different, spend a different currency, speak a different native language, or follow different leadership—and yet be deeply connected to you in fundamental ways.

Alliances form, grow, and reproduce because the global communication infrastructure is a virtual superhighway through which billions of people can connect, share ideas, collaborate, and learn from one another at any time, all at the same time. People are aggregating, joining their voices, and addressing societal challenges in ways never before possible. Some of these people have been underrepresented or even voiceless throughout history. There's a new source of power emerging, to be sure. It is yours and mine, and it is ours together. There are unintended consequences, having both positive and negative effects.

We're already at a point in history where connection and collaboration no longer require introductions or physical spaces. As these interventions become relics, new platforms replace them. More and more, we are members of a connected society, partners in the workforce, and a community ripe to create change. We are swayed by the voices and ideas of leaders from traditional and nontraditional corners of the world. New generations of leaders are growing up in this empowered, boundaryless reality.

The same technology that has opened the doors to new alliances, connections, and communication also provides a platform to advocate unlike any in history. The news is always on and coming from distant corners of the world. Social media platforms amplify voices speaking on important issues. Greater numbers of people spanning place, culture, age, language, and status have ready access to a way to hold leaders and each other accountable.

Voices Carry and Connect

It started with a blog. It was 2008, and BBC Urdu was attempting to better understand how the Pakistani people lived under Taliban rule. To fill in details, it looked for a schoolgirl to blog anonymously about her life in Mingora. The courageous eleven-year-old Malala Yousafzai volunteered.

Under the pen name Gul Makai, the then seventh grader wrote about how the Taliban were destroying schools and banning education in her hometown. She shared how the atrocities were affecting her. BBC Urdu posted Yousafzai's first entry to the blog on January 3, 2009. What followed was a ten-part series titled *Diary of a Pakistani Schoolgirl*. In it, Yousafzai described what she was seeing and how it made her fear for the future. Before the Taliban began to rule her Pakistan town, she had loved school and learning. She dreamed of being a doctor.

In raising her voice and sharing her story as part of a way to demand change, Yousafzai risked her life. She was fifteen years old when the Taliban shot her in the head as retribution for speaking out against the oppressive edict that girls were not allowed to attend school. They did not succeed. The horrifying event brought attention to a global issue that indirectly affects most of us. Approximately 260 million children around the world lack access to any type of formal education. Girls are most impacted by the lack of opportunity—they represent 54 percent of the unschooled population in the world. While heartbreaking and scary on its own, the stats are made more pressing when you realize the lack of opportunity feeds a growing population of almost 780 million illiterate adults.[7]

In 2014, Yousafzai became the youngest person to date to receive the Nobel Peace Prize. She was seventeen years old. During her Nobel Lecture, her strong and direct call to action was to fight against the forces that deprive children of education: "This award is not just for me. It is for those forgotten children who want education. It is for those frightened children who want peace. It is for those voiceless children who want change. I am here to stand up for their rights, to raise their voice. . . ."[8]

The real power of technology as a tool for communicating, collaborating, and creating impact is evident in the fact that it only takes one voice to expand our aperture and get traditional leaders to take note. Like Yousafzai, young, mighty force Greta Thunberg is another one of these voices. Her story is a perfect example of how an unexpected stakeholder, taking unexpected measures, captured the attention of global leaders and ended up adding human energy to the worldwide debate.

In August 2018, sixteen-year-old Thunberg sat every day for three weeks outside the Swedish parliament in an independent protest focused on climate change. A few short months later, she stood courageously before world leaders at Davos 2019 with a call to "hold no bars." In a matter of weeks, Thunberg went from Davos to leading the day of #schoolstrike, when an estimated 1.4 million inspired young people in 2,233 towns and cities across 128 countries stepped out of schools and into the streets to add their voices to hers.[9]

Thunberg is now a living legend. In a little less than a year, this young climate change activist ignited a global youth movement. With her conviction and message, she raised awareness and action for a cause vital to life on our planet. She proved, without any doubt, that one voice, magnified by technology and spread across boundaries, can mobilize others and reshape value systems and social norms.

The kind of public action and systemic disruption created by young people like Yousafzai and Thunberg creates social influence because it is *human-driven* and *amplified by connectedness*. In large and small instances across the world every day, people are organizing and energizing movements. Technology is the tool. Humans are the energy. Using shared social platforms, people are finding one another and banding together to achieve shared objectives. Unfortunately, we also see that people unite for nefarious purposes. Consider that the very tool that these young women used to amplify their voices and mobilize others is the very same platform that exposes others speaking out to abuse and repression.

Hyperconnectivity has disrupted typical organizational structures, erased communication barriers, and opened bottomless vaults of information. The layers and silos that once provided tidy categories for behavior are coming down. The web has expanded the pool of potential connections, allowing people to identify and relate more on experiential and ideological similarities, regardless of their shared geographic, demographic, or generational backgrounds.

Of course, the hope is that individuals act responsibly and use this connectedness productively. Governments must respond to, represent, and engage this proliferation and diversity of voices. Business leaders have an imperative to see and act on the market challenges and opportunities of this new reality. Organizations of all sizes and types are operating in human-centered markets with human-centered entities capable of inciting and creating world-altering impacts. These dynamics show no sign of reversing, and organizational resilience will require that leaders adopt new mental models of transparency, trust, and truth.

Shifting toward Human-centric

It may sound like simple common sense to state that taking full advantage of the world-altering impacts of human energy requires leaders to keep people at the center of their organizations. Yet this is an active commitment that means we have to accept the heuristics, assumptions, values, and ways of interacting that each of us bring to the community. Every environment is unique, for better or worse, because of its human quilt. It's what ultimately shapes the culture of an organization—and that culture is critical to that organization's resiliency and success. The better you can tap the strengths of people, the healthier your organization will be.

The idea that culture is an aspect of business performance has been around since the introduction of Dr. Elliott Jaques's work *The Changing Culture of a Factory* in 1951.[10] However, it's only in the last decade or so that leaders have intentionally endeavored to create culture by clarifying the behaviors and norms needed to succeed within their organizations. The idea behind the commitment is a good one. It ties people and purpose to outcomes. It is powerful when the culture aligns around a shared objective, ideally one with a positive impact on humanity.

Human-centric means optimizing the organization around the people inside and outside the organization and the relationship between them, rather than allowing process or structure to dictate decision-making. Adopting and nurturing a human-centered organization requires structuring a culture that promotes agility, trust, and risk-taking. It allows for fluid thinking and the collaborative, purpose-driven personae that populate the modern workforce. Top-down models that prioritize structure and process fail on every level. These striated models hinder creative problem-solving and dampen the energy of those in the organization who desire to make a difference. You risk the relevance and resilience of your organization if you neglect to understand and facilitate the fundamental need to connect and belong.

The reality of that risk looms urgently. Extensive Gallup research on global employee engagement between 2010 and 2020 consistently shows that more than 80 percent of employees worldwide are *moderately to actively* disengaged in their job.[11] While the data varies across aspects such as region, position, and education, the point is that most companies have yet to realize the potential of those who work for them. The statistics tell us that more than half the workforce is psychologically unattached to their work and company, even to the point of being resentful. In a true Pareto principle (80/20) situation, it leaves the enthusiasm, ownership, performance, and innovation necessary for progress to a small segment of the organizational population.

We can see the situation as depressing, or we can see it as a tremendous opportunity. Leaders in knowledge-based industries may be more likely to find that their employees are engaged in their work than leaders whose employees perform more routinized roles. It makes sense. Knowledge workers have more opportunities (and expectations) to voice their ideas and opinions, to expand their skill sets, and to use a unique combination of strengths and experiences. However, even in these environments, there is more that can be done.

As we move deeper into the Knowledge Age, the shift to more knowledge-based work generally could mean more people have the opportunity to be engaged at work. Even in traditional industrial environments, conditions and expectations have loosened to allow the workforce to contribute intellectually. But amending the systems is no guarantee of satisfaction. Regardless of the type of organization or role, if employees remain indifferent, they will not bring energy or passion for the job, nor will they help their companies grow and pivot in dynamic markets. If you cannot quell dissatisfaction and disengagement, you may see your company increasingly struggle to innovate, create, and compete. As we have seen day after day in the media cycle, mobilizing an entire movement can begin with a single voice. And that force can work for you or against you as you try to compete in a dynamic and unrelenting market.

The Human-centric Modern Organization

Being human-centric is a form of active intentionality. It starts by looking outside the organization, appreciating humanity, and seeking to make a difference. It then builds shared values, behaviors, and objectives that align to a higher purpose. Leaders of human-centric organizations recognize that even if their company has the best tools and processes, people are its reason, meaning, and significance. They value people above all, optimizing around individuals rather than allowing structure and process to dictate strategies and decisions. When disruptive changes happen outside their organization, they understand that real, productive problem-solving and engagement come from empowering people, wherever they are in the organization. They talk about and tap into human energy as a source of power and differentiation. The human-centric organization, then, is one that continually cultivates its people and measures that success culturally, as well as in its business performance dashboards.

The human-centered model is not new, though the terminology used to describe it has evolved. Early in the twenty-first century, the systems scientist Peter Senge attracted attention in management literature, psychology, and organizational studies with his concept of the "learning organization," an entity in which people continually expand their capacity to create the results they truly desire. It is a culture that nurtures new and expansive patterns of thinking, where collective aspiration is set free and people continually learn to see the whole together.[12] It is, essentially, a human-centric organization.

Then and now, succeeding with this model requires that individuals in the group fundamentally understand the relationship between themselves, the larger organization, and the world in which they operate. They know their relationship with the problem at hand or the opportunity they're chasing. Everyone in the team shares the awareness, and there's little to none of the command-and-control management model that persists across so many of today's corporations. The expectation of a free flow of ideas builds trust and confidence. Without a shared appreciation for the ecosystem and its goals, even the best of intentions likely will result in little more than the status quo.

Leaders cultivating human-centric organizations understand this balance. They are keen to be part of the things they are seeking to change. They know that anything besides genuine investment of care and intellect is likely to result in frustration and resistance from those inside their organizations. Everyone within a human-centric organization is connected and valued.

Nurturing a human-centric model must not be seen as a task on a corporate to-do list. It isn't a change management program to deploy and measure progress. It is a behavioral change that goes to the fiber of the organization. It demands embracing a set of shared core beliefs and behaviors. And all that requires that you clear out unneeded, even harmful, antiquated ideas about connection, communication, human potential, and leadership.

With increased understanding of human energy and human-centric leadership—and the courage to take bold, experimental steps—you will begin to see real progress.

This work is challenging, but technology offers the tools to tune in to humanity and listen more closely. As you do, the voices you hear will help you to understand more deeply and to embrace more broadly the positive energy of humans.

chapter two
The Human System

When a society is hit by a wave of technological change, it is often forced to reexamine its beliefs... The society may find that certain long-held beliefs are simply irrelevant or out of date.

—Alvin Toffler, *The Adaptive Corporation* (1985)

A couple of years ago, my son and I traveled to Paris, France. We had been before, but always on short layovers. This trip was different. It was our chance to spend time delving into the beautiful historic city. Our expectations were simple. We wanted to see the major sights, enjoy the diversity of food, and walk everywhere. Our agenda included the Musée d'Orsay, the Musée du Quai Branly, and, of course, the Louvre. These visits covered miles of galleries filled with paintings, sculptures, and artistic artifacts like tribal celebration masks, totem poles, and coronation jewelry. Every part of our planet was represented, from Oceania, Europe, and Africa to North America and Asia. The collections cascaded through millennia.

One reason this trip was so meaningful was that my son is an artist. He observed skills, genres, and techniques, color palettes, formats, and contrasts. His educated perspective brought depth I'd never considered to the works. Because I lack an artistic gene, I was less attuned to technique. What I did see were countless shared patterns and connections. Thousands of works of art, from a wooden carving of the Madonna by an unknown Oceanic artist to Sandro Botticelli's *Young Lady with Venus and the Graces*, to Muhammad Charif Musavvir's The *Reader* all resonated with a common thread.

Humanity.

Over and over, across eras, cultures, geographies, economies, and political structures, these works of art told stories of
people. Even in the most ancient pieces, my son and I connected
with the artists' expressions of family, life, struggle, love, faith,
conflict, birth, and death. Each piece was proof of shared experiences and a reminder that the human condition binds us. No
matter the highs or lows, geographies, cultures, or even eras,
we are one.

Our actions as individual human members of a shared global
community burn brighter than any other point in history,
largely because of the technology conduit that connects us all.
As it has throughout history, our story is unfolding moment by
moment. What do you think the human story will look like a
century from now, hung on the walls of the best museums? I
have a feeling that if we strip away the markers of the era, the
works of art will convey the same evidence of humans fully
engaged in challenges, emotions, and connections with others.

The System of Systems

Our hopes, dreams, desires, and basic needs make up a human
system that binds people together. This has always been the
case. Our connections are real even though the complex, connected global environment we live in continues to evolve
through the decades. Because we are so hyperconnected, the
potential for sweeping consequences and disruptive impacts
grows exponentially. Interrelated systems like politics, economics,
environmental issues, and business shape our collective and
individual lives. Many of these systems seem to operate outside
of our control or input.

The world is a *system of systems* that swirls around and between
us, impacting our decisions and outcomes. We feel the influence

of these systems every day. Whether we're doing mundane tasks like buying food or putting gas in our car, or we're navigating more impactful decisions like choosing a health care provider or putting money in retirement savings, we interact with a system. And each of those systems has its own size, boundaries, processes, decision-makers, and tempo.

For the most part, we don't understand these systems. We may not even sense they exist. Yet we try to build controls. We evaluate the results of our interactions with them. As we do, we often find that the results of our interactions with human systems are not what we expected and maybe not what we desired. The one thing we do know is that our lack of insight limits our ability to assess possible outcomes before we make a final decision. It's human nature to strive to manage our lives a little better so we can create some stability and be able to envision control over our cause and effect. Put simply, we each want to exert control over the systems in which we live and operate.

Your Business and the System of Systems

We each live and operate at the nexus of many macro and micro systems. For example, a business is a system in and of itself. It also is a system of systems. It has purpose and motives, and it develops internal systems to support them. In fact, leaders spend much of their time working to optimize systems inside their business to achieve performance goals. We see examples within organizations:

The Financial Organization: Leaders construct processes and gather resources to equip the company's financial system to manage the flow of capital inside their business and to work effectively as part of the external global economic system.

The Supply Chain: The supply chain system ensures that necessary supplies are available for product and service development inside the organization, and the system works with external relationships to prevent disruptions and streamline the flow of resources.

Human Resources: Perhaps the essential system for business operations, human resources is critical for qualifying, hiring, monitoring, training, and terminating employees to provide personnel capable of delivering their assigned organization responsibilities.

Much of the day-to-day work of a business is to focus and refine internal systems and to ensure that connections with external systems are carefully managed for target outcomes. The performance, market position, and resilience of each business depend on how well it performs these actions.

Considering the Larger Human System

So what happens when we look past the boundaries of the environment we can know and control? Can we comprehend the larger human system in which our immediate (e.g., business) system functions? Likely not. Even while we know we are part of a shared existence (the timeless artworks in Paris showed us that much), we lack the breadth of vision and connection to truly understand our place in the system of systems. To control our present and shape our future, we need that clarity about our relationship with one another (system), our community or industry (system), our society (system), our culture (system), and our humanity (the largest system of all).

As we try to control things around us, we lose sight of the fact that our shared humanity is fundamental to progress. Our connectedness creates volatility. Disruptive system interactions can cause stress. Uncertainty about the future and what steps to take can rattle us. All these feelings of uneasiness with unpredictability can cause us to take actions that are counter to our business and stakeholders.

Instead of giving in to the unease, you must give precedence to the human system that encompasses and connects to all the others. You must stand in the place of human concerns and needs, meet people where they are, and only then begin to make decisions for your businesses.

Does the Flap of a Butterfly's Wings in Brazil Set Off a Tornado in Texas?[13]

The search to quantify the unpredictable effects of complex relationships and interdependent systems has challenged scientific and philosophical communities for decades. But it was research on weather patterns that would become the founding principle of modern complexity theory, which is key to understanding the impacts of the human system.

In the 1960s, Dr. Edward Lorenz was a meteorology professor at the Massachusetts Institute of Technology. His focus was on creating models that could forecast the weather. By studying the effects of different conditions such as air temperature, air pressure, wind speed, and humidity, Lorenz observed that even small changes in different variables could significantly influence future weather forecasts. Lorenz's work became known as the "butterfly effect," based on his suggestion that the flap of a butterfly's wings had the power to cause a tornado. The theory of complexity was born.

Scientists in such fields as biology, ecology, meteorology, mathematics and computational science, and engineering have worked to understand the messiness and seeming randomness of nature and humans. Because of their efforts, we have gotten a better understanding of such things as the genome, immune systems, social media network behavior, and the economy. All are systems within systems. Each has numerous micro-interactions within its larger organizational system and then even more interactions with a greater, more encompassing system.

This networked ecosystem and butterfly effect have shaped modern business management and operations.

Butterflies in the Boardroom

Incorporating complexity theory into business management practices helps you anticipate risks and seize on shifts that may create new opportunities. The exercise should also remind you that, even with the best strategy, external impacts are going to exist and you cannot control everything.

As the business environment has become increasingly dynamic and competitive, it has become more unpredictable and complicated. Globalization has taken hold, all but erasing geographic, cultural, and economic boundaries. E-commerce *is* commerce, completely changing the way we think about customers and competition. New, disruptive business models for delivering value to global customers are proliferating— because they must. The demand for transparency has become louder and more regulated, putting exponential pressures on businesses. Hyperconnectedness has raised the level of risk that one decision will have impacts on society, the environment, and humanity at large. As that's happened, the communities in and around our businesses expect more, again raising the stakes on every decision.

The business agenda now must regard matters that were once the sole purview of global causes. Issues including the aging population, low birth rates, the dominance of the millennial demographic, hyper-segmentation, disenfranchised young people, loneliness, and depression have become part of the corporate agenda.

In an attempt to spin all these large, fragile plates, leaders have aimed their focus on what they can control or at least influence. Most of the time, those factors are "owned" by internal departments or some ancillary structure related, but not directly central to, the business. While the feeling of a tight sphere of control may provide some comfort, the complexity of our global systems means that these efforts increase the risk of failure because they are akin to putting on blinders to the outside world. If you are focused on the resilience of your business systems and the systems in which they operate, widening the aperture is essential and urgent.

As businesses strive to keep pace with ever-accelerating market dynamics, their challenge is only growing. The internet has connected us and ushered in a new chapter in the story of progress. Connectivity continues to prompt waves of new global risks and concerns for humanity. With every new wave, organizations will have to rethink and revise the relationships they have outside their immediate boundaries to keep their place in the system.

In this environment of broad, sweeping shifts, it's harder than ever to anticipate and evaluate courses of action. This challenge is where being a human-centric leader moves from concept to practice. Once you embrace the value of becoming a human-centric leader and shift any perspectives holding you back from that capacity, the next step is to identify the necessary changes. With those hard tasks done, you can begin to assemble the tools and techniques to create the leadership capabilities and organizational structures for a new operational reality.

This whole introspective process actually begins with an external viewpoint. We start by working to truly understand the broad set of people with whom we must interact and communicate. And that requires we put aside any definition of *stakeholder* as merely a customer or prospect. We must spend the time to map out the complex, interdependent system of systems networks and consider the people who are part of our internal and external communities that matter to sustaining our business, thinking from the most local to fully global standpoints. This headwork is critical to lay the groundwork for a human-centric perspective. And it is not a singular, conclusive effort. A sustained analysis capability that focuses on people in every decision is necessary for the resilience of human-centric organizations.

Serving the Needs of Every Market

It was on a trip to Uganda to track mountain gorillas that really drove home the consequences of connectivity and the need for human-centric views of growth markets.

Traveling to Uganda is not easy. Getting to the area where mountain gorillas live is even more challenging. My launching point in Uganda was Entebbe. It's roughly 450 miles from Entebbe to the Bwindi Impenetrable National Park, the home of the mountain gorillas. You can travel by car, bus, or plane. Going by bus or car takes about eleven hours (on a good day), assuming no vehicle breakdowns along the way. By plane, the trip is somewhere between a two- and three-hour flight, depending on the number of stops required to pick up and drop off passengers. That number of stops is decided only a couple of hours before each scheduled flight, because actual departure, arrival, and flight times depend on last-minute ticket sales. If there's a silver lining, it's that the transport plane for the route holds only eight passengers. I got lucky. The day of my trip to Kihihi airstrip, the flight took two hours.

My guide picked me up in a Jeep cruiser from the short dirt runway. He set the expectation that we'd travel approximately two hours to get to Bwindi, my lodging point for the next few days. He apologized ahead of time for the condition of the road and the dust we would experience. His description understated the reality of the trip. We traveled on a dirt road that had been severely washboarded from the rainy season. A thick dust cloud surrounded us most of the way.

We passed buses full of people and trucks with goods. Every now and then, we would pass a small village with half-dressed kids playing with dogs or goats. Every village had a small area where people traded goods such as coffee, bananas, and tea. Most of these people transported their goods from village to village on foot. We passed women walking between the villages with containers for water held on their heads. My guide told me that people sometimes had to walk as much as fifteen miles to gain access to drinkable water from village wells.

Once we reached Bwindi Impenetrable National Park, my close encounter with mountain gorillas was life-changing. (I could spend the next few pages discussing these amazing creatures, but that is not the point of this story.) The wildlife, geography, community, and commerce were illuminating. But the humanity I encountered on my last day in Bwindi completely shifted my worldview. I saw firsthand how decisions made by businesses in other parts of the world happened without sufficient understanding that their impact could spread to corners of the globe like this.

I decided to get a massage from a woman named Dembe. Like me, Dembe is tall. During the massage I made a comment about her pretty sandals. She thanked me and lamented how hard it is for her to get shoes that fit her size twelve feet, especially any shoe that is pretty or feminine. I naively asked her why it was so hard. Plainly, she described the incredibly random supply chain that brings goods like shoes to her village. Without access to the internet, the people in this village lack choice. They have no proactive means to access things they want or resources they need.

It was clear to me that connecting people like Dembe and those I saw living and working in the small villages on the road to Bwindi the internet would be a good business proposition. There are some three billion people who have yet to be connected via a communication infrastructure, even as satellite companies work hard to fill those gaps. For businesses that lack a human-centric viewpoint, it would seem to be an enormous opportunity for profit. Once accessible, someone like Dembe is an ideal prospective customer.

But there are realities to this scenario more important than business growth. Access to computers is a rarity and the electric grid sporadic at best. Even if they could get online, most don't have jobs that pay enough for them to buy goods. And, recognizing how many tedious steps it took to get from the airport into these small communities, even if they could order goods from the internet, getting them would be a herculean effort that could take months or years, not days or weeks.

Sandals aside, many people in the world, like those I met in Uganda, don't even have ready access to clean drinking water. It raises the question: As our businesses work to expand markets, are we considering what the point of this effort is? What critical global issues must be addressed to sustain the very markets we are attempting to create? And how are we thinking about them with regard to our growth strategy? How will we ensure the execution of our plans doesn't have unintended consequences that create negative impacts on the communities we want to interact with? Addressing these questions is human-centric leadership.

Network Exponentials

Since 1983, the point at which the "network of networks" launched the modern internet, humanity has become so linked that today, globalization is a pervasive reality that we generally take for granted. The sphere has broadened so widely that most companies regularly, aggressively, and simultaneously address local, domestic, and international demands. Opportunistic strides increase the amount and variety of choices for customers, which raises the level of competition and prompts disruption in product and service markets.

In many economies, this constant demand-supply-innovation-competition cycle drives down the price of goods. Lower prices open new markets in countries that historically have been less economically advantaged. Systems collide, intersect, and grow as that expansion happens. And so continues the cycle of human connection.

While this networked system is robust among goods and services sectors, it is still maturing in a few areas that are critical to human survival. Waves of innovation, price, and accessibility decisions like I saw in Uganda continue to fail to consider society's broader needs. Even as leaders build plans to get goods to new markets and consumers, they tend to overlook foundational priorities like clean water and air, quality food, and safe communities where children can go to school and parents can earn a fair living wage.

As the internet has exposed our shared humanity, we have become more aware of these needs. Citizens are turning to global civic and business leaders to do something. That something begins with considering the human system inside their organization and the system that comprises their customer base, as well as the global network that overlays and connects them all.

The intricacies of the human system and the business system are vast. Each connection point in these systems has the potential to represent and influence exponential impacts to environmental, social, geopolitical, and financial considerations, among others. Some of those outcomes, like innovation markets, are opportunistic. Others, like the devastating results of climate change, forced cultural migration, cyberattacks, food shortages, water crises, and pandemics, represent global-scale risks.

We're only just beginning to really understand the extent to which the decisions and actions of businesses impact people. And that understanding is exposing the ways in which human consequences create issues for businesses. It's a cyclical situation with cascading effects.

To a large extent, we have yet to develop the tools necessary to see beyond the interfaces we deal with on a daily basis. We don't have the resources to identify and manage all the known and unintended complexities. We're aware of these forecasting gaps. It's a reason businesses work to align and structure functions and control mechanisms. By limiting the variables, we hope to improve our ability to control performance.

But as soon as we consider the *human* system, it blows those controls wide. We open the business up to the influence of a broader set of opportunities and threats to mitigate.

Consider the term *surveillance capitalism*, coined by Shoshana Zuboff in her 2019 book, *The Age of Surveillance Capitalism*.[14] During her book tour, she asked, in one word, why attendees were interested in the subject of her book.[15]

The responses were telling. People used such words as *fear, manipulation, control, intrusion, misinformation, mistrust,* and *privacy*. These words describe a rising collective concern about the negative consequences of hyperconnectivity. Businesses have developed the capacity to harness the free flow of data produced as people coexist with technology. Zuboff describes surveillance capitalism as a unilateral claim on data about our private human experiences—raw material about what we will do now, soon, and later that is free, exploitable, and easily monetized. It's how companies create the products and services they bring to their "users." Zuboff observes that a powerful backlash is coming.

It's hard to predict what this counterforce to hyperconnectivity and data will look like, but one thing is certain: companies will rush to develop and market new products and services in the area of personal privacy.

Imagine, for example, an offering that combines insurance and brokerage services that represent individuals and secure their pattern-of-life data. On one hand, we will be able to classify data by what we want to protect, what we don't care if others use, and what we would like to license to others. These new security products and services will help us protect our data and broker licenses with companies with whom we are willing to share our data in exchange for income streams. It could move us toward a more balanced relationship between us connected consumers and the companies seeking to benefit from our behaviors.

Understanding the consequences of the counterforce of humanity as it pushes on the momentum of technology and existing business practices will help us move toward becoming a human-centric organization. We know that it's necessary. We also know we're not prepared and, in some cases, simply unwilling to make changes. What to do?

In the absence of a checklist or instructions, the best way to proceed is to illustrate by example. What are the considerations and questions that organizations are asking as they step into the human system to look honestly at their business?

A Water Treaty That Affects Us All

"It is in the interest of all humankind that Antarctica continue to be used exclusively for peaceful purposes and shall not become the scene or object of international discord."[16]

Travel is my passion. As my list of trips has grown, the destinations have gone farther off the beaten path. A trip to Antarctica pushed those boundaries to their farthest reaches.

The original intent of my voyage was deeply personal. In that regard, the journey did not disappoint. The idea of traveling to Antarctica started with a desire to reconnect to my father, who passed away in 2005. In the early 1980s he worked at McMurdo Station, the U.S. research center on the southern tip of Ross Island. His efforts added to our global communication capability. My decision to travel on board National Geographic's *Explorer* to this amazing continent was to share, in some small way, what he had experienced so many years ago.

What I did not expect was how immensely it would add to my professional perspective about human-centric leadership. Intellectually, I have always understood that Antarctica does not belong to any one country. Until this trip, however, I didn't fully appreciate the importance of the arrangement. Nor did I really understand the impact of the Antarctic Treaty.

On December 1, 1959, twelve countries signed the pact to protect the continent as a scientific preserve and ban military activity. Today, fifty-three countries have signed the treaty. No sovereign nation has a claim on any part of the Antarctic territory. The continent is dedicated to peace, science, and all humanity. In every way possible, the agreement holds a delicate ecosystem in balance that, if disrupted or destroyed, could have devastating impacts that extend to our very survival.

Antarctica is a hidden, natural critical infrastructure for Earth. Whether we know it, our lives rely on it. Unlike the roads that we drive on, the financial system we expect, and the internet we take for granted, Antarctica is not commonly known, understood, or even seen. Only about fifty thousand people have the opportunity to visit each year. It is far away, difficult to reach, physically taxing, and prohibitively expensive for many. Antarctica is a major player in the human system, despite its distance from our daily lives. Each of us is connected to this wonderful place by our shared interdependence on water and climate stability and by our decisions that ultimately impact its ownership and use.

The continent is 98 percent ice and only 2 percent actual land. It covers approximately 5.4 million square miles and contains roughly 6.4 million cubic miles of ice. These numbers are almost incomprehensible—it is the biggest single mass of ice on Earth. Approximately 90 percent of Earth's fresh surface water is held in the Antarctic ice sheet.[17] It's that fresh water that forms the otherwise unlikely connection to the Coca-Cola Company.

It's difficult, perhaps impossible, to think of a brand more globally impactful and universally known than Coca-Cola. Since its beginning in Atlanta, Georgia, in 1892, the company has grown its portfolio to more than five hundred brands. It operates approximately 225 bottling companies and a global distribution network of more than eighty-four thousand suppliers. In the United States alone, the company sells more than eight hundred beverage varieties. Almost two billion servings of Coke are consumed every day, seven days a week, 365 days per year. The company generates over 70 percent of that business income from non-U.S. sources. With more than seven hundred thousand people in the Coke business network, the corporation is a genuinely complex, human-driven business system with virtually limitless connection points.[18]

The magnitude and breadth of the organization are stunning, but the relevant point here is this: Coke started branching out internationally in the 1920s but began its global expansion only in the 1980s. Over the past several decades of Coke's globalization endeavor, company leaders have learned the hard lessons of complex interdependent business systems.

The challenges and lessons of doing business in multiple countries include more than language barriers, geopolitical perspectives, legal standards, cultural norms, conflicting time zones, and regional nuances. Evolving global issues like climate change and access to clean water add a magnitude of complications for Coke as it works its way to the future.

As an example, climate change impacts the world's water in complex ways. Alternating temperatures in Earth's atmosphere impacts its water cycle. Warmer air holds more moisture than cool air. It absorbs that water from oceans, lakes, soil, and plants, leaving less water for drinking or for agriculture. As the warm, wet air cools, it creates rain and snow. A warmer world means heavier rain- and snowstorms. While in some parts of the globe, massive precipitation seems like it would be beneficial, heavy rain is hard for the soil to absorb. A warmer atmosphere also causes more rain and less snow, which means less snowpack. Snowpack is nature's way of storing water for later use. It essentially "hides" water from evaporation. As winter snowpack melts in the springtime, the process slowly adds fresh water to our rivers, replenishing drinking water supplies. Less snowpack means less drinking water.

While it seems like thinking about how climate change affects Earth's ecological systems is adjacent to Coke's business operations, the intricacies and relevancies are massive. There are approximately six hundred ecological systems on the North American continent alone. Scale that number globally. That's countless biological communities that share similarities in their physical environment and that are influenced by regular ecological events like fire or flooding. Climate affects each of these systems, impacting the water sources in each one.

Clean, high-quality water is the essential ingredient for hundreds of beverage companies that do business around the world. The industry uses an estimated 150 billion gallons of water annually. Coca-Cola is the most significant player. Alone, the company requires around twelve billion gallons of water per year just to stay in business.[19] It obtains this water from myriad sources and systems that cross city, district, county, state, and country borders where it maintains distribution and customer spaces.

Governance of water is a political, social, economic, and emotional challenge. The issues of water management are very fragmented. It is a system of multiple interrelations among natural resources such as soil, fauna, plants, and humans. Who gets what water, when they get it and how, and who has the right to related services and benefits are an entangled lattice of policies, legislation, and institutions across government, civil society, and the private sector.

As a global player, Coca-Cola is doing business in the middle of all these considerations, discussions, and disputes. Its interdependencies are the definition of complex. It must manage water relationships across a vast number of countries. The competition for clean, usable water isn't limited to other beverage companies—it comes from everywhere.

Experts and major competitors within the water, agriculture, and energy sectors have no obvious incentive to collaborate. Nor do they have the leadership or framework to facilitate collaboration. The agriculture sector makes decisions that impact water availability. Different parts of the world have varying approaches that may conflict with each other. The water sector makes decisions that affect energy use. All these external individuals, organizations, frameworks, and industries impact how Coca-Cola makes decisions and operates.

Climate change is completely reshaping global water resources and the industries that depend on them. Beyond being the primary ingredient in beverages, water access has consequences on the availability of sugar—the second most crucial ingredient in a Coke. For the company, all this means that the task of sourcing these two central ingredients is monumental. At the end of the day, the same environmental concern that affects Antarctica places Coca-Cola right smack in the middle of one of the hardest problems facing humanity.

Water access is perhaps one of the most fundamental human issues. It *should* drive all beverage companies to take a human-centric approach to their business. In truth, the water issue should prompt most companies operating in the global supply chain to consider their place in the human system. It's significantly more than a resource that comes from a faucet, pipe, or local service. Water is necessary to virtually everything, and there are no alternatives. It's fundamental to our food supply, the drugs that keep us healthy, even the silicon chips we need for our electronics. When the tap runs dry, as has happened in major cities including Cape Town, São Paulo, and Chennai, it impacts lives, livelihoods, and businesses—not just in those cities, but around the globe. And it can create war.

If the water issue is so prevalent and fundamental to survival, why do only about 10 percent of today's companies have a water management strategy? Even for those that do, many fail to harness the complex interconnections that extend beyond the boundaries of their company. If we see the business as one player in a series of larger human-centric systems, perhaps we will understand the gravity of decisions like water negotiations as more than a piece of the supply chain. Avoiding a tragedy of the commons must be a priority.

Coca-Cola has a proactive water management stance. It must. But it goes beyond the supply chain implications. The company promises to return 100 percent of the water it uses to make its products. Is that commitment enough to secure all the interdependencies across the human system? Can we really know that Coca-Cola considers remote places like Antarctica and its relationship to it? In time, we'll know.

The governing treaty that has secured this pristine and powerful place will come up for possible renewal in 2048, leaving it vulnerable to modification. Nonetheless, a few countries and companies have already begun to make arguments for opening the treaty to allow for drilling, mineral exploration, and mining. If these allowances occur, they will accelerate the impact of climate change on the already melting glacier and ice sheet. Looking nearly thirty years ahead, many see opportunities to exploit the untapped Antarctica resources to support their own agendas. But what is the point of competing for these resources if they become irrelevant because of the profound negative impacts caused from extracting them on customers, societies, and humanity?

The consequences will be severe for us all.

Antarctica teaches us that we have limited resources and they must be protected and shared. It is the perfect example of a harbinger of our planet's wellness. We are all interconnected in the present and future health of this place. Nothing is too small or localized to help with our global challenge. Leaders must prioritize understanding these intricate connections and make business decisions that balance human considerations and the human system. Humanity is the system in which all others exist—it is the only ubiquitous platform.

chapter three
Recognizing the Chasm

Leaders who attempt to redesign old institutions face denial, stubborn resistance and conflict. Innovators who seek to create new institutions or organizations face skepticism. Both need guts, political skill, tenacity, a sense of timing and commitment. They need allies.

—Alvin and Heidi Toffler, *Revolutionary Wealth* (2006)

I love working with executives who are determined to transform their organizations. So many of them share qualities that position them to be powerful and positive leaders. They are passionate. They have a gut sense of the disruption happening in their markets. They see how industry boundaries are blurring to create new competition. They understand technology is at once an equalizer and a differentiator. They intuitively know they must make hard decisions today to secure the future viability of their organizations. Their inherent sense of urgency drives them to search out new ideas and business opportunities for a successful future. And they are known for taking action and are intolerant of resistance to necessary change. They know change happens through empowered people.

These types of executives are rare. More common are the executives who are aware of the urgency we face with respect to convergence, know hard decisions must be made, and yet are unwilling to make them. Their public persona can often be "visionary" or "change-making," while behind closed doors it is a different story. They are resigned to their organization's path and are working desperately to maintain the status quo (and the approval of shareholders). They hide behind process and structure instead of grappling with being a human-centric company.

I once worked with the CEO of a large, complex enterprise with a globally recognized brand. Let's call him Robert. Services for the company were centralized within the headquarters, and the product and service lines shared financial performance accountability. The company's largest revenue-generating business was a legacy commodity, which was battling declining profit margins. In an attempt to capture new markets, the company had made a string of significant acquisitions over the course of a couple of years. The actions added growth to the company, but not to the level that shareholders expected. As the company continued to miss performance goals, its leadership responded by adding layers of oversight.

Robert understood the company must produce products and services to meet the needs of *tomorrow's* customers. But he also sensed that any effort to innovate new offerings was getting harder within the existing organization. While the external imperative existed to position the company for the future, Robert was unwilling to disrupt it from the inside. He feared what may happen if he exerted too much power to meet the challenges they faced. Even when I questioned him on his leadership, he had excuses that always had a clear correlation to the structural limitations of the organization. By keeping the organization the same, it also remained accountable for its failures, rather than Robert. The personal fear of failing could not be overcome, making it impossible for Robert to hold himself accountable and to challenge his company to do better.

We know that Robert is not unusual. His challenge is true for many leaders. And when it comes to considering a company's human-centric role, which may counter perceived benefits to shareholders, this fear of disruption becomes all the more entrenched. Without a larger set of values driving a company's goals, the motivation for leaders like Robert is naturally one of self-preservation, for both the company and themselves. They don't want responsibilities that transcend the company. And they don't want to break anything. But the reality is things are already broken.

We have evidence that the capacity and willingness to focus on the human element may well be the quality that defines our most successful leaders. Contemporary disruptors like the celebrity chef, restaurateur, and nonprofit founder José Andrés are driving decision-making and strategy that withstands even the most complex and abrupt change.

Andrés is the exemplar of a human-centric leader. His passion for what he does and for whom he does it is clear. He is a rare combination of compassion and business entrepreneurship. He came to America from Spain when he was twenty-one years old. Two years later he partnered with Rob Wilder and Roberto Alvarez to create Jaleo, one of the first commercially successful tapas restaurants in the United States. His career as an award-winning chef took off. Over the next several years, he opened dozens of successful restaurants.

Until around 2006, it seemed as though Andrés was driven mostly by his gift as a chef and a powerful entrepreneurial spirit. It was at that point that he cocreated ThinkFoodGroup with Wilder. With more than thirty different types of restaurants in its portfolio ranging from two Michelin-starred restaurants to a food hall, ThinkFoodGroup dedicates itself to not only creating culinary experiences at every price point, but also giving back to the communities and the world it inhabits. Its singular mission is to "change the world through the power of food."[20]

Andrés has proven himself as a world-celebrated chef, a successful businessman, and a humanitarian. In the past decade, those human-centric proclivities seem to have driven his decisions, and they are picking up momentum. In response to the 2010 Haiti earthquake disaster, he formed the World

Central Kitchen. The nonprofit organization operates on a mission to "create smart solutions to hunger and poverty." At the time of this writing, the organization has delivered over forty million meals in more than four hundred cities around the world. By bringing freshly made, hot meals to those in need, the World Central Kitchen disaster relief teams deliver important nutrition and subsistence to the hungry. But they also bring a message of hope.

Maybe it was his early experiences as a chef in the Spanish navy that gave him the ability to be agile, but wherever it came from, he learned to sense and act quickly. In 2017, when Hurricane Maria devastated Puerto Rico, Andrés went to the small island to help. He did what he does best: he cooked. When asked how he could step in and feed so many in a place where there was no water, electricity, or grocery stores, he responded that his capacity was fueled by the urgency: "It's a very simple thing when you're a cook. When you are hungry, you gather the food, you gather your helpers, you begin cooking, and you start feeding people."[21]

Rather than get overwhelmed at the thought of having to feed more than three million people on the island, he segmented the challenge into what World Central Kitchen could accomplish. First, cook for twenty thousand people. Once you can do that well, then scale up to cooking for forty thousand people. Don't let existing structure, policies, or procedures get in the way of doing what is needed to get done for the future.

When the pandemic hit in early 2020, Andrés again pivoted quickly. As people were asked to stay home and quarantine, he shut down all his restaurants in Washington, D.C., and New York to turn his attention to doing what he could to help people in need. Again, World Central Kitchen stepped in, transforming closed establishments into community kitchens, part of a nationwide effort to feed those in need with low-cost or free meals, always made from fresh, never prepackaged food.

Even while we admire Andrés for creating the nonprofit, many leaders may decide the model isn't one they can emulate because they have shareholders to prioritize. Certainly, they may want to do something like the World Central Kitchen, to make such a generous impact, but their shareholders demand financial performance first and foremost. Generosity and charity are a privilege, and not one many of them feel they can give in to. Andrés obviously disagreed with that notion and created a way to answer both his shareholders and his value system. He is intolerant of the status quo.

His umbrella entity, Tapas Holdings Inc., is valued at roughly $50 million.[22] He has more than thirty equity-holding investors. Those shareholders hold Andrés and his leadership teams accountable for the financial performance of all the restaurants in the diverse portfolio. Rather than keeping a myopic focus on the demands of investors, Andrés has channeled equal amounts of passion and creativity on profitability and on addressing people's most urgent needs. In fact, one of the tenets of his mission is profitability, because, as Andrés articulates, "profitability leads to possibility."[23]

Today, businesses are born with a capacity to grow globally at breakneck speed and to be rendered obsolete in an equally unprecedented time frame. Products and services once considered enduring are now questioned, both by (skeptical) customers and (anxious) producers. Shifts are constant, significant, and interdependent. Each one demands that we be willing and able to understand and address changes with wisdom, agility, and calculated haste.

Radical changes are happening in every sector and across social, geopolitical, financial, and even environmental spheres. In the last quarter century alone, we have seen the formation and weakening of the European Union, the rise of e-commerce as a global economic foundation, self-driving cars, e-books, augmented reality, commercial genetic testing, 3-D printing of human organs, multiuse rockets, and artificial intelligence (AI) taking on human jobs. A global pandemic forced us all to reevaluate how we connect, work, trust, travel, and spend. Thousands of other disruptions are reshaping the world around us. Each disruption creates a ripple effect on business, the economy, civilization, and the world.

Production has shifted from an era of industrialization and mechanization, during which mass production and quantifiable efficiency reigned supreme. For decades, characteristics like standardization, order and discipline, and task-driven processes by human labor constituted the central definitions of a successful business. No more. Corporate survival depends on networks, demassification, customization, innovation, agility, and, perhaps most important, human intelligence and human energy. The shift has profound implications for businesses and the people in them.

Leaders like Andrés are showing the world it's possible to succeed by keeping people at the forefront of every decision and action. They possess rich insight nurtured through courage, empathy, tenacity, and clear core values. They prioritize people, integrate technology to meet and advance needs, and shape operations around higher-value objectives and emotional intelligence.

What lies ahead is not for the weak or hesitant. We must leave behind current business structures and operational principles that have run their course. Crossing the chasm to an emerging and, in many cases, still-to-be-created way of doing business will take humility, courage, and resilience.

Changing Mental Models

Mental models are beliefs about how things work. Established and ingrained through our interactions with the world, they offer frameworks through which each of us organizes information and creates building blocks of knowledge. With mental models, we are able to process knowledge through belief systems to understand what's happening and why.

Supporting the transformation to a human-centric organization will require leaders to adopt new mindsets with new mental models about business. We will need to reexamine and update organizational designs that worked in the past, along with the mental models that guided those approaches. This endeavor will be hard. Our mental models are integral to who we are as professionals. We have imprinted thought processes and decision-making behaviors through time and experience. And these deeply set mental models prioritize the business system over the human system. But the momentum of technology development and its convergence with humanity's needs demand we try. When we do, disruptive, creative thinking prevails.

The evolution of Wikipedia offers a case in point.

In 2000, Jimmy Wales and Larry Sanger launched Nupedia. They envisioned a free online encyclopedia with high-quality articles that would rival *Encyclopaedia Britannica* or *World Book Encyclopedia*. Their first step was to assemble a group of academics that could churn out accurate and authoritative content. Next, they set up an advisory board consisting of Ph.D. experts from across various academic fields. Then they instituted a rigorous seven-stage online review and content approval process that closely mirrored the rigorous review process of scholarly journals.

The Nupedia business model focused on quality and authority, with a heavy process and approval cycle. After six months, Nupedia had only two full-length articles. At eighteen months in business, the number had grown minimally, to twelve. The platform was stagnant. In September 2003, Nupedia closed, having published only a meager twenty-four articles.

The same rigorous processes and quality standards that defined Nupedia had created barriers to its growth, because they prohibited everyone outside of the small academic community from contributing. Wales and Sanger had used a model from the past, not pausing to challenge their beliefs about the market or how the organization must be structured and governed. They didn't consider how people were changing and what affect this might have on their business. They were not even aware of the old mental models they brought to their new idea. They failed to look into the future and notice how the market was shifting, neglected to consider what new human-centric models must exist.

Soon after Nupedia's failure, Wales and Sanger took another swing at creating an online encyclopedia. Taking what they had learned, they started again with Wikipedia. The platform and company have gone on to achieve everything Nupedia could not, likely because Wales and Sanger had a clearer understanding of the potential for the internet to become a platform where humans could collaborate. They developed Wikipedia with five simple principles that could guide a continuously evolving organization: 1) Wikipedia is an encyclopedia; 2) it is written from a neutral point of view; 3) it is free content that anyone can use, edit, and distribute; 4) editors should treat each other with respect and civility; and 5) Wikipedia has no firm rules.

Wikipedia has succeeded because it emerged from a human-centric perspective. It has continued to grow because it is free of hierarchical command and control. Rather than a heavy adherence to structure and process, it allows leadership to emerge throughout the entity. Wales and Sanger spotted and overcame existing mental models about what an organization should be. In doing so, they created a new model of knowledge sharing and erased long-held convictions about governance, structure, and process.

Wikipedia is only one example of an organizational platform designed with a human-centric mindset. Many businesses are shifting their primary focus from products and services to value-based interactions and connections. The movement is relevant to the evolution toward human-centric organizations because these models are, in effect, forums where people can interact purposefully. Networked and platform-based business models are gaining importance concurrently. While varied in structure, platform organizations create ecosystems that connect people, facilitate interactions, and engender diverse communities of shared purpose and mutual trust. Those are fundamental human impulses that can drive incredible business potential. For example, LinkedIn gains value as more people join, interact, and contribute. Airbnb provides access to people with needs to people with valued assets. And when Amazon shifted from being a reseller to being a marketplace, it opened doors for others to actively engage their customers within its platform, hence contributing to the company's growth and financial performance.

Mental models tend to support an incremental mindset: if we do what we are currently doing, just better, everything will improve, and we can make progress. Shifting our mental model from business first to human centered requires a transformational change.

The Shifting Intent of Business

Once we recognize that we must embrace new mental models to change, we must start the process by addressing a fundamental question: What is the primary intent of our business? As we've seen in this chapter thus far, the predominant business-first mental model would say that its sole purpose is to maximize profit for shareholders. That idea has driven corporate decision-making processes since Milton Friedman introduced it in the 1970s.

It's not surprising that this concept has endured. It is simply constructed and easy to understand. It allows us to hone corporate decision-making in a fast and furiously dynamic market by quieting stakeholder demands (such as the cacophony of wants and needs coming from the human system). It allows us to zero in on making money, rather than being more broadly tuned to employee concerns, changing customer values, and societal issues. This determination makes running a business more comfortable, no matter how big it is.

A few leaders and organizations have kept from falling in lockstep with Friedman's concept. Throughout the years, those voices have contended that money is not, in fact, the true purpose of business. For example, students of Peter Drucker share his position that "if we want to know what a business is we have to start with its *purpose*. And its purpose must lie outside of the business itself. In fact, it must lie in society since a business enterprise is an organ of society. There is only one valid definition of business purpose: *to create a customer*."[24]

Throughout his long career, Drucker voiced strong beliefs about institutions, including the idea that businesses must live up to their responsibilities to society. Drucker's pursuit of the common good is shared by another human-centric leader: Peter Georgescu.

In Georgescu's 2017 book, *Capitalists, Arise!*, the longtime business executive argues against reports that connect economic growth with the overall economic health in the

United States. To support his challenge, he and his colleagues processed a wide-ranging set of statistics across varying aspects of the economy. They intended to show that corporations that focused solely on a few shareholders rather than a broader set of stakeholders actually harmed the economy. If people cannot make a wage that supports a basic standard of living, they cannot spend money on consumer goods.[25]

Georgescu's study looked beyond the stovepiped data of stock prices, productivity, and economic analyses geared toward reporting shareholder returns to the world. His experiences in marketing and advertising trained Georgescu to understand people's hopes, dreams, and desires. He built his career on the ability to tap into the human system. Looking beyond the economic reports to observe people raised the question: If the economy is growing and we as a nation are doing better, why are so many people hurting?

The simple answer that must be considered is that the narrowing concentration of corporate America on shareholder primacy has hijacked free-market capitalism. We have optimized our business systems to match this prioritization.

The idea that leaders must manage corporations to maximize shareholder value began to take root in the 1980s, around the time Friedman's influence was on the rise. Before this time, corporations tended to act as though they owed something to the community that provided them an economic ecosystem in which they could grow and thrive. Little by little, that benevolent, civic belief disintegrated, making the nature of business more global and more competitive. Multitudes of new performance enhancement initiatives (like algorithm-driven decision-making mechanisms) positioned the shareholder—not customers, employees, suppliers, or the community—as the central purpose of business. The supremacy measures moved beyond the confines of individual enterprises to reshape what constituted economic wins as well. Most of us don't remember this transformative era; most of us grew up in a business system that had already shifted.

Over the past four decades, the expansive system that promotes shareholder primacy has become a significant cause of inequality and angst across the human system. Georgescu warned of unintended consequences from economic inequity between a few and the masses. He predicted that continuing on that path could destroy economic prosperity and possibly even our democracy. And he was not the only one sounding the alarm.

On any given day, we hear leaders echoing Georgescu's concern that something just isn't right. Growing numbers of guests on mainstream business outlets from Bloomberg to BBC to *Squawk Box* and others are asking hard questions about business purpose and focus. They're challenging their peers to answer: What are we giving back? How are we solving the problems in our communities? How will we be able to continue to operate among the shifting sentiment of customers? Does the value we provide as senior executives warrant the salary we receive?

Despite the countering voices and questions, most business leaders remain under Friedman's influence, whether or not they realize it. It stretches as an undercurrent across articles, business podcasts, and MBA curriculums. We hear it in our conversations. We repeat it among ourselves. Those who aspire to move into corporate leadership commonly recite the idea that the company's main purpose is to take investments from shareholders and creditors to generate profits.

We have come to an important crossroads. Is the sole responsibility of the business to contribute to shareholders? Or does it also include contributions to the broader spectrum of humanity in and around it? How we answer those questions is essential in determining how companies and leaders go forward. The answers will decide whether we are willing to transform the organization, or if we'll keep the organization as it was developed in the past, whether or not it still fits.

Leaders committed to building and nurturing companies capable of changing the world understand that business is about more than making a profit and catering to a limited set of shareholders. Making money is imperative for a business, but we have to take a broader view. Doing so starts with asking a fundamental question: How can we continue to make money if we neglect the needs of our human system? The question may seem straightforward, but the answer is anything but. Ultimately, the needs of the human system hold the key to creating revenue.

We need to ensure that our decisions, and the decisions made by the companies we lead, reflect the influence and impact of people. The momentum of shareholder expectation of financial returns is powerful. We must understand those influences and, above all, ensure the organization cares for and nurtures the market and its environment. Doing that requires that we factor the human system into our business decisions and actions.

Serving stakeholders is different from serving shareholders. And if there is no environment in which to do business, there is no business. Even once we acknowledge the reality of that assertion, the hard part is overcoming the momentum of the past decades and shedding outdated (and even detrimental) mental models. Despite their declarations to the contrary, most organizations are not actively human-centric.

It's possible to evolve. Getting there will require that organizations fight against the current momentum of the status quo, and that will require redoing even basic organizational systems. We must rethink how we take in information about the environment, process it inside the organization, decide what to measure, and outline the decisions and actions we must take. Then we must iterate, challenging and re-creating output results to confirm they satisfy the human system's needs.

The Divergent Organizational Hierarchy

While many parts of the modern business scenario feel unprecedented, they are not. We can learn from critical points in history when the emergence of new technologies caused the corporate organization to evolve. From the late 1700s to the late 1800s, the Industrial Revolution took hold because automation capabilities and assembly lines galvanized mass production. New tools and processes emerged to solve a resource need as companies turned their focus to speeding mass-produced products to eager customers. Organizational management became a top-down model. We stood on platforms of consistency, standardization, compliance, reporting, efficiency, and performance.

Early in the twentieth century, the American mechanical engineer Frederick Winslow Taylor took the top-down model a step further when he developed a scientific management practice to improve industrial efficiency. He recognized that employers could maximize efficiency within their factories if they broke labor projects into parts and trained their laborers with specialized skills.[26] His tenets were far-reaching and influential. They changed how we interacted with people within production processes. It was an organizational construct that served shareholder primacy, and as such, it fit its time.

A management model like Taylor's practically guarantees fragmentation, overspecialization, and a need to control from the top. It succeeded because of its dependence on two factors: heavy and accurate feedback from the field and relative homogeneity in the types of decisions required.[27] Taylor believed that employees were motivated only by money. He didn't believe that workers could enjoy or get satisfaction from their jobs. These biases led to the development of heavy monitoring and controlling processes that made sure employees were productive for the business. There is limited space inside this model to consider the human system.

As its fundamental conditions for success disappear, and we recognize the importance of a human-centered organization, this structure and leadership formula is slowly losing value in knowledge work businesses. However, Taylorism is still followed to keep costs as low as possible in businesses that are trying to remain competitive in labor-intensive industries.

As part of its strategy to keep the average price of a meal low, McDonald's practices the Taylor model. The quick-serve chain operates more than thirty-seven thousand restaurants that employ approximately 210,000 people in 120 countries across the globe.[28] Each restaurant looks alike. The instructions to cook a burger are exactly the same. Even the guidelines for cleaning the floors and eating areas are mechanized. By breaking jobs down into small, consistent pieces, these restaurants, like others in the fast-food business, operate at a high efficiency.

Although strict adherence to Taylor's management model has become progressively outdated as the rate of change, complexity, and connectivity intensify, we still see market leaders like McDonald's using a top-down management structure. The organizations are structured around clearly defined lines of authority and a tight span of control. They continue to measure success by task productivity and output volume, not necessarily by ideas, collaboration, or problems solved.

Part of the reason we have not succeeded in making a full transformation is that our efforts to flatten our organizations and take down structures that hinder human energy for innovation and problem-solving have fallen short. The communication tools we have implemented, the integrated product teams we have created, and the streamlining of processes we have instituted have not gotten us to where we need to be.

Even though we advanced from the Industrial Age to the Knowledge Age almost half a century ago, most current organizational models continue to function as vertical hier-archies optimized to deliver shareholder returns. The model is less adaptive, more restrictive, and unlikely to reflect the human-centric mindset vital to innovation and progress. While many of us profess that we do have a collaborative organization that practices inclusion and values people, the data presents a compelling counterargument: 80 percent of employees worldwide report they are moderately to wholly disengaged in their job.[29]

The takeaway for leaders is that most of the people within your business are not helping the organization achieve success. Imagine the impact if those team members operated as such. What could you accomplish if the people working in your business were inspired to support its purpose and objectives, and then worked with that intent?

Pyramids to Pancakes

Even as leaders strive to flatten organizational models, the world has already accomplished an incredible shift. Humanity is consuming, accessing, creating, enriching, directing, and sharing a constant undercurrent of digital data. Information and communication technologies are rapidly imbuing every element on the planet with some measure of computing power and a network connection, absorbing them into the expanding global information network. Roads and bridges, miniature satellites, personal devices, plants, animals, and even our bodies are tagged with tiny, low-cost sensors connected to advanced networks locally and globally. That's only going to become more normal.

The connections between people, between things, and between people and things are enabling unimaginable new forms of value creation and competitiveness. The result is a sense of boundarylessness that has and will continue to change the rules. We're seeing evidence of an actual human system that includes every one of us and is in a constant state of ebb and flow.

These emerging networks of people and things are creating new knowledge at a rate that wildly surpasses forecasts. Man-machine teams are becoming the norm throughout business. The global data share is becoming ever more essential to societies, individuals, and businesses. From using data to predict whether someone will get cancer to solving complex traffic flow issues, the ways we can use the global datasphere are expanding—and will continue to grow as the creation of new data begets the creation of new data. It is incumbent on us to know the people within our organizations and how work is distributed within the man-machine team. Being human-centric means making sure humans are ready to realize the full benefit of technology.

As we enter the second decade of the twenty-first century, we're coming to a point where every one of us on the planet interacts thousands of times each day with digital devices.[30] Every interface between a connected digital device and a human generates new data and insights, which birth even more connections. The process continues in a perpetual cycle, widening our networks and producing profound consequences for the transparency of information and on the systems of business.

While most of us would not argue the implications of this hyperconnectedness on business, few consider how it is shaping human evolution. And yet, we must. Each new idea has the power to influence and direct how countless people think and behave. We know that those behaviors have consequences on everything from microeconomies in Uganda to climate change in Antarctica. And those realities have business implications.

The current pace of global change demands a very different organizational management model from the past, when change was slower and significantly more encapsulated. New decision authority structures are still evolving. What we know is that the modern organizational construct must appreciate and prioritize human energy, fluidity, and action. It must realize that the new technologies that we are implementing inside our businesses are giving us incredible opportunities to revise how we set and execute decisions. As all this future unfolds, we need to ask courageous questions, like how we should reorganize authority structures within business to optimize the productivity of new human-machine teams. We need to examine and reset decision thresholds and consider the consequences of crossing them. We need to identify and agree on who has the authority to take new operational steps and how long their authority should exist. Doing so will flatten and push authority and responsibility from the pinnacle of the organization through to the outer edges of our companies, harnessing human energy to improve business performance.

At the moment, the *who, what,* and *how long* of authority and decision-making are not being considered at a pace that can keep up with the development of advanced technologies. It's yet another reason for the human-centric organization. The structure will enable leaders to develop new management behaviors for direction and execution that are more attuned to the needs and motivations of the human-machine teams in order to achieve the higher corporate objective.

Reaching Organizational Transformation

An organization is like a civilization. It is a complex network of connected people who sense, analyze, communicate, and problem-solve. Connections with others inside and outside the organization act like platforms for our professional, local, and even global communities to share perspectives, beliefs, interests, and solutions to problems. That is, if we encourage this to happen.

Albeit expansive and deeply entrenched, the human network remains underutilized. Fortunately, a cultural shift is under way. Unfortunately, the change is not widespread. It recognizes each individual in the organization as a thinking, producing, and mindful contributor to its goals and success. Leaders play a critical role in driving progress by putting intention toward how their business operates independently and interacts outside the organization, inside the organization, and between one another to accomplish high-level outcomes.

Dr. Brené Brown cautions us to slow down and take note of possible consequences of our actions: "When the culture of any organization mandates that it is more important to protect the reputation of a system and those in power than it is to protect the basic human dignity of the individuals who serve that system or who are served by that system, you can be certain that the shame is systemic, the money is driving ethics, and the accountability is all but dead."[31]

Drucker, famous for the tenet "culture eats strategy for breakfast," likely would have applauded Brown. Both of these human-centric leaders push us to see the direct correlation between healthy company culture and its positive business performance. To be successful in the future, businesses must balance the time spent on developing strategies and action plans with building strong, healthy cultures.

They must work to close the chasm between business first and people first.

Doing that hard work takes the willingness and courage to commit to overcoming any lingering beliefs that the sole purpose of business is to maximize shareholder profit. Even as you see wildly successful companies operating on old profit-first mental models, emerging case studies of human-centric organizations like Patagonia or Ben & Jerry's should encourage you.

There's no doubt that Friedman continues to influence shareholder-centric decisions and practices. It's up to you to acknowledge the extent to which that focus defines your organization and how much you're willing to do to change the mental model in order to forge a different path forward.

Globalization is no longer a "new" normal, and the flow of information and ideas has become a constant reality. Businesses intent on resilience have no choice but to anticipate and prepare for converging paths. You must deliberately and relentlessly pursue the conscious decision to serve everyone who has a relevant relationship with your organization, instead of putting sole focus on shareholder profit. An excellent place to start is a systematic change within your business to put its people first.

chapter four
Decision Disruption

To survive today's onrushing changes, we must be prepared to reconsider
the very models on which our obsolete organizations are based.
—Alvin Toffler, *The Adaptive Corporation* (1985)

Working with hundreds of organizations in the public and
private sectors has given me a deeper appreciation of the
spectrum of complex challenges organizations face. Operating
environments of government institutions, nonprofits, and
business enterprises are increasingly affected by internal and
external forces that change almost overnight, posing significant
issues for those responsible for execution.

Many of us struggle with the demands of strategic and
operational decision-making during times of great innovation
and societal evolution. We struggle to acclimate to a world in
which humanity is demanding we take a lead in solving the
world's hardest problems—decisions that must consider the
health of our business and our responsibilities to stakeholders,
which can be daunting. When decision-making becomes harder,
a self-preservation instinct can kick in. A default reaction to
do *something* can result. We must be aware of gravitating toward low-cost, high-noise signals as a substitute for genuine
reform. To ensure the survival of our organizations, real action
must create sustainable and meaningful results. Real action is
more than new corporate slogans, PR campaigns, or knee-jerk
reactions taken to make an example out of an employee.

The CEO of Gravity Payments, Dan Price, is a leadership
legend before his time. As a young entrepreneur, he had the

vision and courage to replace outdated mental models in his business with decision-making that had people at its center.

Price founded Gravity Payments to give small business owners more affordable options for processing customer credit cards. He prided himself on how he prioritized his employees and treated them fairly. He thought he was succeeding in his purpose—until a brave employee brought up Gravity's salary structure. While competitive for the market, the salary at some levels within the company, especially entry level, was not enough to cover even minimal living expenses. The frustrated employee called Price out for talking one way but acting another. It set Price back on his heels. He could have let the encounter go, sticking to his position. After all, he was the founder and CEO, which gave him a leadership vantage point and insight about the company and industry others lacked. Instead, Price listened. He took a careful look at his company.

The employee, it turned out, was correct, not just about the salary structure but also that Price's actions did not match his rhetoric. Price had to agree. More than that, he took action. His decision-making process and bold changes could not have been easy. He didn't have many role models to help him set the course. He acted outside 2014 business norms, earning chastisement from other leaders who said he was responding to a catastrophic environment that didn't exist. But Price followed his gut to put people first and ultimately created action toward becoming a human-centric company.

For the next three years, Price gave Gravity employees annual raises of 20 percent to begin normalizing a new salary structure. He began phasing in a minimum wage of $70,000. In a bold move, he cut his salary by almost 94 percent, from $1.1 million to $70,000, to help fund the payroll shift to his employees. His actions now aligned with his words.[32]

Over the next four years, Gravity Payments flourished. Profits grew. Gravity's payment processing went from $3.8 billion in 2014 to $10.2 billion in 2018. The company increased its staff from 120 to more than 200, adding talented executives including Tammi Kroll, a Yahoo executive who took an 80 percent pay cut to become Gravity's COO.

In early 2020, faced with the COVID-19 pandemic crisis, Price's actions to level salaries became a true testament to the human value of his decision. Faced with a drastic downturn in business resulting from people staying at home, many without jobs and lacking discretionary funds, Gravity had to make a critical decision about its future. Price was determined not to lay people off or raise prices to survive. Unsure of how to accomplish those commitments, he asked his employees for ideas. They came with the recommendation to voluntarily cut their pay. They would weather the crisis together.

As of this writing, it is still unclear what lies ahead for Gravity, but all evidence points to a healthy company culture where values are lived out with consistency and passion. When leadership exhibits clear human-centric values, these values will be ones that tend to be shared by all employees.

Capital markets are shifting fast. They too are signaling the prioritization of human-centric organizations like Gravity. For more than a decade, the United Nations has backed the Principles for Responsible Investment (PRI) initiative. It launched in 2006 with sixty-three investment companies committed to incorporating environmental, social, and governance (ESG) issues and corporate social responsibility (CSR) initiatives into their investment decisions.[33] The original signatories totaled $6.5 trillion in assets. Within twelve years, the community of signatories grew to 1,715 and $81.7 trillion in assets—well more than a 1000 percent increase in participation and investment dollars in just over a decade. The global investment analysis firm FTSE Russell has confirmed that in 2020, more than half of global asset owners are implementing or evaluating ESG considerations in their investment strategy.[34]

One of the earliest and most influential voices in this process is BlackRock CEO Larry Fink. The world's largest asset management company, BlackRock had almost $7 trillion worth of investments under management at the beginning of 2020. Fink used this powerful, far-reaching platform to boldly raise his voice, calling for all leaders to stand aggressively on ESG issues. Since then, his messages have become an increasingly clear and courageous rallying cry for responsible long-term business strategy. Backed by some of the most influential contemporary leaders, Fink has become a powerful force for our future and the future of humanity.

In a discussion with the Economic Club president David Rubenstein in April 2017, Fink described what he called an epiphany that he had around 2012.[35] It was roughly three years after the buyout of Barclays Global Investors, which included the iShares index fund. It was then when he realized that BlackRock was the ultimate long-term investor. By owning all the companies in the fund, BlackRock had a stake in their outcome. As long as their performance was healthy, the company stayed in the index. If not, BlackRock had a responsibility to help them become successful.

BlackRock created a corporate governance team to provide underperforming companies with support and guidance needed to improve performance. The intent was not to pressure company leadership into making short-term gains. Rather, it was a long-term strategy. In his annual letters to his portfolio company CEOs, Fink shared the need for a longer-term approach to business. He also applied the method and commitment to helping solve the hard problems of humanity.

Fink's letters to CEOs have evolved since he first started sending them out in 2012. The first letters were cautious communications. They did not attempt to instruct companies on how to act. Instead, his approach was to request engagement on governance mechanisms and consider the positive implications of strategies for delivering future and long-term value. Over time, four themes emerged: good governance, outward focus, purpose leadership, and climate action.[36]

When Fink started getting serious attention from a few forward-thinking leaders, he grew more direct with his observations and calls for action in these four areas. He has pressed harder for leaders to look outside their organizations and to proactively consider environmental and social factors in their corporate decision-making. He has explicitly highlighted the need for business to meet external stakeholders' interests and to have a broader purpose in society. He has called leaders to action to spearhead resolving social and environmental issues. The challenge has brought strong pushback and criticism from the status quo.

In his 2020 letter to CEOs, Fink threw down the gauntlet. He projected the voices of a broad range of stakeholders, not just those who owned stock, including the BlackRock workforce, members of the local communities where the firm operates, and individuals within the larger global society. His message was loud and direct: "We are on the edge of a fundamental reshaping of finance" and as such have a fiduciary responsibility "to help clients navigate this transition."[37] Specifically, he argued that many companies have yet to recognize the critical need to address broad stakeholder implications. As divisions continue to happen around the world, leaders must demonstrate their commitment to the countries, regions, and communities where they operate.

We're only at the start of a vital, sweeping movement from the ingrained prioritization of shareholders to a genuinely inclusive, activated focus on stakeholders, and there's much to be done. Even as adoption and engagement slowly increase, organizations are struggling to figure out how to integrate a higher purpose of business into the corporate operating system. To remain resilient over the long term, leaders must embrace a new model for how their companies define a successful business. And it won't be easy.

Fink's challenge to solve today's hardest ESG issues gets strong pushback. Contention arises from those who believe movements such as CSR or sustainable business practices (SBP) distract leaders from their core obligation to act in the best interest of shareholders. Nonetheless, Fink persistently prods leaders to go beyond merely discussing (or even implementing) do-good corporate programs. He calls them to rewire their corporation to be human-centric and focused on stakeholders. For example, climate change is central to his message. He points to the fact that we must consider climate as a defining factor in long-term prospects for economic growth and prosperity.

In short, Fink is asking us to incorporate the human system into our businesses. Along with a growing throng of other disruptive leaders, Fink contends that this responsibility is as obvious and straightforward as prioritizing the broad spectrum of stakeholders. As we've seen in the efforts to shed Friedman's tenets, however, becoming a human-centric organization is complicated. It's a foreign move for many. It forces us to rethink why and how we make decisions, keeping in mind the much broader needs and implications of all people, not just the ones accounted for in the customer and investor lines.

The True Definition of Efficiency

To help us rethink our decision-making processes and behaviors for the future, it is instructive to look back and see
how we got to where we are today. It was almost a hundred
years ago that Chester Barnard introduced the term *decision-
making* into our business vernacular. He was working with
communication systems at AT&T when he published his
theory of modern organizations in his 1938 book, *The Functions
of the Executive*.[38] He viewed organizations as systems of
cooperative human activity and proposed that the survival
and longevity of an organization were dependent on two
criteria: effectiveness and efficiency. We are all familiar with
these concepts, but perhaps not in the same way that Barnard
conceived of them—efficiency in particular.

Most of us would agree with Barnard's definition of effectiveness as a means to assess an organization's ability to
accomplish its stated goals. We might take issue with his ex-
planation of efficiency as the degree to which an organization
can satisfy the motives of the individuals within it. This
definition is human-centric. When he introduced it, his concept
of efficiency differed from many others, mostly because they
were implementing Taylor's model.

Whether we realize it, Taylor has had more of an influence
on most of us than Barnard has. We spend time conceiving,
implementing, and measuring efficiency in the organization
through plans and strategies that expend the fewest possible
resources for the greatest financial gains. We place massive
amounts of attention on searching for or building business
structures capable of delivering ideal shareholder results.
We refine processes to align all parts of the organization
to accelerate strategic outcomes and shareholder profits. We
search articles, podcasts, and business bestsellers for new

Deborah Westphal

ways to hone efficiency. We hire consulting firms to assess our operations and give us feedback on how we stack up to industry benchmarks and how we can improve. We bring in change management organizations to communicate our desired efficiency goals, tailor employee job descriptions for clarity of responsibilities, and bake in execution behaviors across the organization. We outsource functional responsibilities such as our IT in the name of improving efficiency. We track and report daily, monthly, and quarterly efficiency metrics. If we miss the mark, we create action plans to get us back on track as quickly as possible. We nurture a culture of efficiency. Ironically, it's exhausting.

True, we justify most of this activity as necessary to running a business. The danger in it is that our actions are propagating an outdated model of shareholder supremacy. Maybe even without realizing it, we're putting massive amounts of effort and activity into building tremendous momentum in the wrong direction. Unless we're working toward a top-down, industrial-era success model, these operational efficiency efforts won't get us to where we want to be in the future. That path is trodden by those—like Barnard, Fink, and Price—who show us the value and necessity of a broader inclusion of stakeholders.

Redefining efficiency with people in mind begins with figuring out what kinds of ingrained systems, practices, and beliefs to squelch. We need to get rid of those old models to create space for new activities geared for the human system. Once we have identified the changes and embraced disruption, we can start to cement and measure new efforts. The process won't be easy. We may even think that it is a poor fit for our current organization, determining that we should leave it to our successors to tackle. But given the intensifying demand for businesses to take on more responsibility related to ESG issues and the time it will take to pivot onto a new stakeholder primacy path, we need to start now.

It took several decades to ingrain the mature organizational model that dominates today's marketplace. It will take time to reexamine why Barnard prioritized human motives for the future success of an organization and what efforts we need to continue, modify, or cease. One particular task comes immediately to mind: challenging the assumption that technology will improve our decision-making capabilities.

In the twenty-first century, public, private, and government entities have raced to innovate and implement technology on the promise that it will speed decision-making and free people to do higher-value work. Some may. But it's just as true that many of these technologies actually may increase the very gap we need to close if we are to move into the future with productive, efficient human-centric organizations.

To illustrate the point, in a 2016 article for *Fortune* magazine called "The Hard Evidence: Business Is Slowing Down," then CEO of the Corporate Executive Board (CEB) noted that despite advances in technology, decision-making in business was actually losing momentum. A CEB work place survey revealed that the growing prevalence of tools designed to increase collaboration within the business was prompting 60 percent of employees to create time each day to consult with at least ten colleagues to get their jobs done. What was more, half of that 60 percent said they needed to engage more than twenty people to get their job done.[39] It's fair to assume that over the past several years, this issue of efficiency has not improved, given the proliferation of new compliance, privacy, data protection, and enterprise resource management tools.

We seem to be replacing human interaction with technology tools, thinking that it will smooth and speed processes. The reality seems to be the contrary.

Dangerous Decision–Making Divergence

A formative and significant divergence is happening within our businesses. There's been an explosive rise in the use of information technologies to enhance business performance. For the most part, it runs counter to the challenge to be more human-centric. No doubt, these resources, efforts, and intent will collide, like the currents flowing around the Galápagos Islands, shaping and reshaping how strategic and operational decisions get made and measured.

Around the world, organizations and people are generating and tapping into volumes of data in almost real time. Technology can organize and exploit it quickly. That may be why so many of us believe that emerging technologies like AI and machine learning (ML) are critical assets for corporate performance and growth.

It's true that technology can process quantities of data faster than the human brain. In that way, it is capable of enhancing business performance. But it's far from a perfect tool. There is a danger in over-indexing on data, AI, and ML and failing to include human system needs in the decision-making processes. Successful use of technology for a resilient human-centric business requires precision, clarity, empathy, and balance.

The challenge is not new. The intoxicating promise of technology has been present throughout history, and it has become more attractive as innovation and change accelerate. The 2020 release of an annual AI survey of more than 2,300 global business leaders illustrates the point.[40] The survey showed a 25 percent increase in the use of AI over the previous year. More of us are looking to bigger data sets and more accurate algorithms to help make better and faster decisions to increase shareholder gains. And the reality is that survey respondents report a return on their investment. More than two-thirds of those asked saw an increase in revenue generation of more than 50 percent. Most of this growth came from implementing AI to help with marketing and sales, product and service development, and supply chain management. They also realized significant reductions in operating costs, much of which came from low-hanging opportunities to automate functions throughout the enterprise.

There's a balance to consider. While investing in technology that promises to improve business performance and maximize shareholder profits, businesses also are feeling the growing pressure to focus on people, the planet, and their stewardship of both. They are being expected to focus on the bottom line and the wider picture.

We have never been able to resist the allure of promising new technology, and now we can no longer ignore the ESG drumbeat. A new convergence is under way.

Increasingly, socially conscious investors are raising the volume on their call to integrate robust ESG strategies into existing company operations. Investors such as KKR & Co., Roark Capital, and, of course, BlackRock are becoming more demanding for companies in their portfolios to make decisions that have the good of the planet and its people at heart. The entrepreneur Eric Ries has launched the Long-Term Stock Exchange (LTSE), the first national securities exchange promoting a long-term focus for investors and companies. The creation of LTSE minimizes the pressure to hit short-term targets and allows for stewardship that stakeholders and society demand.[41] These and other powerful entities are giving voice to our stakeholders. Whether they are employees, customers, or market observers, these stakeholders are assessing the speed and level of the corporate response—and making important investment decisions based on how businesses stack up.

Stakeholders measure businesses on more than earnings reports. They assess value on how well the organization satisfies responsibilities related to global issues such as greenhouse gas emissions, energy efficiency, water management, and waste generation. They look for evidence of healthy, productive relationships with employees, suppliers, customers, and communities. They want details on how the organization considers social issues like human rights, customer privacy, and workplace diversity and inclusion as it makes decisions.

Addressing the broader ESG demands will take new, more expansive data sets. The challenge in meeting this requirement is that much of the data about issues like climate change, water management, and social inequality typically exist outside the organization's normal channels and purview. Even with emerging technologies like AI and ML promising to streamline the ingestion and management of data from enormous numbers of sources, it's up to the organization to provide access to the necessary information and to commit to using the analysis it produces to support its stakeholders. This shift is a significant undertaking. It will require leaders to collaborate with experts in fields of study that may never have otherwise been relevant to the corporate intent. It will take a system of systems approach.

All these new demands are changing the role that the business system plays in the global human system. Satisfying the broader expectations means we must be able to trust that our algorithms can inform wise decision-making and do so quickly. Rapidly changing environmental conditions are increasing our need to manage reactions in near (or actual) real time. Staying ahead of the decision curve is next to impossible, and the pressure to perform flawlessly keeps rising. For organizations pushing to satisfy external expectations and their own imperatives, the promise of data and perfect business algorithms is incredibly tempting.

In the face of all this potential for accuracy and speed, we need to be leery of the promise of objectivity. Data is not free of bias. Pressure to manage risks in an increasingly compressed period is fueling the development and adoption of algorithms that can mimic human cognitive processes. While the intentions are good, they have drawbacks and unintended consequences. Algorithms can't replace humans when it comes to predicting behavior, trustworthiness, and the value of decisions. Because people build and program ML models and AI, the technology output is inherently informed by human behavior.

The burden is on decision-makers to be familiar with the data sets and algorithms we use and the ways in which they were built. Particularly as we take on the pressure to address ESG and CSR issues, it's vital to understand the tools we use in our response models and to ensure that they accurately represent the breadth of our new focus. To be a human-centric organization, a convergence of information, analysis, and stakeholder primacy must occur.

The Decisions That Matter Most

If we are going to succeed in the near term and the distant future, we have to work hard to overcome any lingering belief that the sole intent of our business is to maximize shareholder profit. We have decades of momentum behind the commitment to deliver profit-based business results for those who have a financial stake in the business. Without first redirecting our focus to valuing the human system most, any technology we add will only serve to accelerate progress in the wrong direction.

That is, of course, unless human-centric leaders like Fink anticipate and call attention to the diverging paths ahead.

This is the challenge that matters most. A deliberate decision to serve all people, not only those who hold a share in the organization, must be carefully informed and relentlessly pursued.

We may be seeing the beginning of this commitment. In the summer of 2019, members of the Business Roundtable ceremoniously signed a declaration that the purpose of a corporation has changed. In its "Statement on the Purpose of a Corporation," the 181 signing CEO members declared that companies need to take a broader view of whom they serve. They concurred that it is no longer enough to serve shareholders. They also must deliver value to customers, employees, suppliers, and the communities where they operate.[42] The agreement is a good start, but it is yet to be determined if it is sufficient or sustainable.

Within six months of the statement being signed and published, COVID swept across the globe. It created historic disruptions to every individual's way of life, how we work, economies, and geopolitical structures. Many corporations heeded the call, quickly launching initiatives and efforts to support those in need. It's fair to give credit for those arguably ESG endeavors. At the time of this writing, however, it's too early to say whether the efforts will subside with the pandemic or if they will be actual movements to new ways of thinking and behaving.

As leaders work to determine if real change is happening, they will have to take deliberate action to state and define new goals and openly communicate measures and metrics of success. Transparency is required. Organizations will be expected to provide information about initiatives being taken to rewire their structure to sustain this new, human-focused direction. Likely, the effort will include incorporating ESG data from network partner sources into business decisions and reporting so measurement is consistent across industries and sectors, and it's simple to spot the trade-offs happening as organizations widen their aperture to understand and provide for shareholders, suppliers, employees, the community, and humanity.

This effort is not either-or. At the same time as they are extending their responsibilities to meet ESG expectations, these same organizations will have to incorporate analysis and reporting into traditional business reporting mechanisms, including Securities and Exchange Commission reporting requirements for public companies. Some forward-thinking companies already have taken steps to disclose their efforts to address environmental and social (E&S) issues in their annual reports or Form 10-Ks. Until reporting becomes structured and consistent, we won't be able to measure how well these organizations are improving year over year or performing comparable to the market.

We have crossed the start line. From here, progress will happen as more organizations embrace the systemic disruption in why and how we make decisions. Doing so will position leaders to do the hard work of redesigning the functions and forms of our business for a human-centric future.

chapter five
Overcoming Obsoledge

Whether they are aware of it or not, companies, governments and individuals today base more of their daily decisions on obsoledge—on ideas and assumptions that have been falsified by change—than ever before.

—Alvin and Heidi Toffler, *Revolutionary Wealth* (2006)

It's exhilarating to get a call from a friend asking for help with a business matter. The chance to understand a new problem, dig deep into its moving pieces, and create a path forward is gratifying. Across the spectrum of issues business leaders ask for help with, growth challenges are especially interesting. They represent the opportunity to step into the future, imagine what the business needs to become, and then work backward to decisions that need to be made today to get to that future.

My friend Ken was CEO of a top thirty defense contractor. He called for some support with a major acquisition he was considering. He'd executed more than thirty acquisitions over the course of a decade or so, but this one was going to be different—larger than the others. The target acquisition was valued higher than the acquiring entity. The intent of the deal was to make a future-focused move to evolve the company from an IT services provider to an information solutions and services company.

Ken believed customer demands were driving a need to transform into a different type of company and that the acquisition would satisfy those human-centric demands. His plan was to first define the objective and then align senior leadership around the vision, hoping integration decisions would produce the company he envisioned. There was a lot to overcome on the path to success.

A decade of acquisitions had resulted in a company filled with myriad capabilities, most of which were unfocused and under-differentiated. Because the acquired companies had never been fully integrated, the business lacked a unifying culture. Ken was running a siloed enterprise where dozens of business lines each had distinct ideas, relationships, and capabilities for bringing relevant solutions to customers. As a whole, business operations were finely tuned to respond mostly to requests for proposals. To make things even more difficult, Ken had almost 130 vice presidents, each of whom had his or her way of doing things and expected to be a part of decision-making endeavors.

The corporate conditions were not conducive for success, particularly with such a large acquisition. Yet it was likely the deal would go through because of the economic environment. This was 2019, a year when the value of M&As totaled almost $4 trillion, making it the fourth-strongest year for deal-making since 1980.[43] Macroeconomic conditions were healthy, there was a lot of cash held by strategic acquirers, and interest rates were low. Acquisition generally was considered to be a favorable strategy for filling gaps in the enterprise, accessing new customers, and gaining capabilities for accelerated growth.

Two points bear reminding. First, the financial transaction of an acquisition may be the *least* risky piece of the effort. Second, acquisitions are more likely than not to fail. History proves that it is easy to buy a company but hard to maintain a successful M&A long term. As Ken bemoaned, deeply entrenched beliefs, cultural norms, and ways of doing things can work against the success of the integration as much as they expand the capabilities of the organization. Every year, even as acquisition rates and values rise, concurrent studies put the failure rate of the transactions between 70 and 90 percent.[44]

A smart acquisition strategy takes into account what markets and customers may look like in three to five years. A brilliant acquisition strategy begins with a careful process of defining every part of the company you want to become in the future and then nurturing a culture of people motivated by knowing where they fit into the vision. That approach dedicates the time and space to identify beliefs and knowledge about the market and the organization that have developed over time, going largely unquestioned. That process of highlighting and working to eliminate obsoledge[45] is necessary for moving everyone toward a shared vision of the future. It puts people at the center of the strategy and *then* it works process and structure.

Ken's company already was not keeping up in its rapidly changing environment. The world of acquiring innovation had shifted and the pace of competition was only accelerating. The company needed creative and proactive operational strategies, as well as a culture that would seek out and exploit opportunity spaces. If acquisition meant bringing in more status quo behaviors and "don't color outside the lines" organizational culture, the company could be further prevented from finding agile areas of opportunity. If that happened, it risked becoming further mired in habitual, learned behavior reinforced by antiquated incentive structures.

Urban legends of "why we cannot" instead of "how we can" had been brought into the company through its prior deals. Worse yet, because of the dozens of acquisitions, the catalog of urban legends was vast.

Recognizing that the amount of obsolete knowledge coming into the organization could paralyze its progress, I advised Ken to begin with an effort to root it out before attempting to bring such a wide spectrum of skills, personalities, biases, and behaviors under a single corporate umbrella. Leadership needed to understand that culture, not capabilities, could be the biggest hurdle to the immediate and long-standing success of the deal. It needed a human-centric perspective. The strategic shift had to start by boldly confronting reality and aggressively (even if uncomfortably) eliminating biases and behaviors that would hinder productive innovation.

The same is true when transitioning to a human-centric organization. Years, possibly decades, of entrenched obsolete ideas, biases, and behaviors tuned to maximize shareholder profit exist within our companies. The shift to a human-centric perspective mandates the identification of the obsoledge so that it can be met head-on. Without doing so, overcoming the existing momentum and direction to set the organization on a new path will be almost impossible to do. Ken's desire to become a human-centric organization needed to address this strong resistance.

Consequences of Knowledge

With the pace of innovation continuing to accelerate, knowledge is being created, stored, and shared at a volume and velocity never before seen. It is hard to say how much the world knows or how fast the supply will grow. The speed of knowledge growth is driven by a demand for more and has a corresponding rate of decay. We try to harness this cycle by expanding our capacity to judge the validity of information and then to make more of it, create languages to express it, organize and specialize it, express and teach it, and finally to quantify and disseminate it.

In short, as the rate of knowledge creation accelerates, so does the pace of obsolete knowledge. In 1982, the inventor and futurist R. Buckminster Fuller, in his book *Critical Path*, attempted to create a model for forecasting the rate of knowledge creation across the human system. His Knowledge Doubling Curve (also called the "Buckminster curve") plots how fast knowledge creation happened through history. He noticed that until 1900, human knowledge doubled approximately every century. By the end of World War II, it was doubling every twenty-five years.[46]

Then came news platforms, computers, the internet, and social media.

Today on average, human knowledge doubles every thirteen months. Because learning progresses in a nonlinear, cross-discipline manner, it's possible to segment the growth rates of specific industries and environments. For example, we know that technical knowledge and genetic information double every eighteen months. Knowledge that is related to online information doubles every six months. The knowledge base gained via social media networks doubles *every twelve hours*.[47] How much of this knowledge is useful? How much is obsolete or just plain false?

Even though we've seen it coming, no real precedence exists for this rate of acceleration. The race to create new knowledge for a competitive edge is fast, furious, and unceasing. It demands that organizations develop the capacity to continually ingest, analyze, organize, understand, and employ a tremendous scope of data about economies, societies, markets, industries, and stakeholders.

Trying to manage the excessive (and growing) amount of data flow has moved many leaders to focus on technology. Analogous to Taylor's blueprint for a manufacturing line, businesses are converting data to knowledge using processes, procedures, standardizations, checklists, quality assurance, and oversight. Knowledge is about data, but more important, it is about people. Here's why.

Knowledge is inherently inexhaustible. A virtually unlimited number of people across the human system can use the same knowledge without diminishing its quantity or value. The more people who use a piece of information, the higher the probability that the knowledge will grow. Access to data is no longer a real competitive advantage (but how you use it to transform information into useful behaviors is). Gathering, sharing, and applying knowledge are human endeavors, and we dedicate many of these behaviors to solving the hard problems facing humanity around the world.

Knowledge is inherently nonlinear. Even the smallest insight has the potential to push progress and solve hard problems. The knowledge network is exponential. Every new discovery or idea opens the way for more. As Ahrendts observes, technology is the conduit for this knowledge flow, and people are the energy.[48] Knowledge grows because humans observe, think, connect, create, and share.

Knowledge is hard to contain. Like chaos, it spreads (mostly) unfettered. At every point of connection, knowledge changes the world through discoveries and convergences. People spend most of their time experiencing life with others. Like bees, people pollinate their organizations and societies with ideas and knowledge. This natural process of discovering and sharing knowledge is the heartbeat of the human system.

Knowledge resides everywhere. We hold the most personal insights within our minds. The knowledge that defines an organization tends to exist within the confines of that entity. The knowledge that is truest to humanity at large spreads across the global information network. Because it can spread and multiply without restraint, knowledge can be categorized, but it's nearly impossible to quantify how fast it is being created and rendered obsolete.[49]

With the volumes of information available and the hyper-connectedness in which we operate, humanity is pushing the Buckminster curve. The unparalleled ability to access and share information is empowering people and organizations to know more, act faster, and reap incredible benefits. And we can do those things if we can assess the validity and use-fulness of the information and take steps to filter out what's unnecessary or obsolete. A business requires mental models built to remove organizational clutter and optimize ideas and efforts around the broader spectrum of stakeholders.

Many established businesses (like Ken's organization) end up resembling cluttered homes. Layers of collected capabilities, processes, procedures, beliefs, behaviors, ideas, and information pile up in the corners of the organization. With management changes come new strategies and directions that demand new knowledge about how we should do things. The company progresses and the operating environment gets disrupted, but the business retains old ways of doing things and structural mechanisms.

Rarely do organizations deliberately consider whether or what to discard and keep. They just layer new ideas into the decision-making framework. The result, like a packed closet, is a frustrating, even paralyzing, overabundance of choice. It makes sense that the behavioral patterns and cognitive biases that keep us from tidying our personal environments would carry over into the business world. Businesses comprise and are led by *people*. Just like at home, each person in the organization considers the acts of disposing and organizing with a mix of rational thinking, judgment, and emotion. It takes courage to look past status quo bias, sunk cost fallacy, and loss aversion.

Without intentionally working to set a vision and "tidy up," many of us fall into a habit of holding tight to outmoded approaches and operations. We are burdened by beliefs, behaviors, procedures, structures, and cultural artifacts that no longer serve a purpose. The remnants hinder progress, create confusion and conflict, and get in the way of achieving our organizational goals. Clearing the clutter positions our organizations to maneuver successfully through chaotic, fast-paced disruption to the point of resilience and fulfilled purpose.

Tidying Up Ideas

Information glut is a massive, dangerous burden for an organization. The tidying process begins by identifying ideas that do not serve the business's purpose(s) and the obsoledge that exists across the organization.[50] As facts, data, beliefs, and biases lose relevance, they gain the ability to inhibit growth and innovation. When many "best practice" business concepts sweep through companies like wildfire, they can tamp creative thinking.

Identifying obsoledge and irrelevancies and taking action to clear them from the organization are the first steps toward opening up possibility and laying a foundation for lasting success. This act is critical for a human-centric organization because it determines whether the entity can optimize around people or if it has become so mired in process and structure that human ideas, and indeed people themselves, barely fit.

As described, the "corporate cleanup" seems straight-forward. Yet the act of tidying up processes and beliefs is rarely done. The environment and the people in it are mostly to blame. In the fast-flowing, disruption-prone climate, leaders must regularly cast new visions and launch capabilities and product lines. Mergers, acquisitions, reorganizations, and geographic expansions keep organizations shape-shifting. Even if the leadership commits to removing obsoledge and clutter, they often end up abandoning the effort before it's complete. Urgency takes precedence over strategy.

Another reason these efforts so often get cut short is that it can be hard to spot obsoledge. But it's not impossible. At the organizational level, it often looks like long-held, but outmoded, biases about how to structure and govern the business. It can be seen in status quo behaviors and the "don't color outside the lines" organizational culture that prevents leaders from searching for agile gray areas in which to operate. And it can be spotted in deep-seated beliefs that guide decisions because they feel safe and comfortable.

Not all obsoledge is damaging. It's the ideas born out of a history of oversight, regulation, and constraint that need to be pulled up from the root to free the organization of its "we can't do that" or "we do it this way" mentality that blocks progress with bias, risk aversion, and even misinterpretation. Thoughtlessly repeated behavior and status quo response threaten innovation and agility.

Capable leaders know how to spot dangerously archaic beliefs and ideas, and they have the courage to clear them out of the way. These leaders have done the work to be informed, bold, and risk tolerant. They replace fads and outmoded cultural beliefs with innovation and human-centric behavior that serve the organization's unique purpose. Seasoned leaders, informed by success and failure, are the cornerstone of nec-essary cultural transformation.

Deborah Westphal

Though the agency has been around since 1972, Pentagram still offers a stellar example of such bold, forward-thinking leadership. Pentagram is the world's largest independently owned design studio, lauded for its excellent work and unmistakable reputation. It is structured as a democratic organizational entity that operates free of hierarchy. Partners have the same voting rights. They actively seek feedback on their performance and creative work from one another and from junior designers. They nurture and perpetuate a culture where issues are aired and solved openly. As a partner exits the studio, he or she commits to seeking a replacement who will add to the company's capabilities and diversity.

With humans at the center of the agency's structure and the work it produces, leadership is able to ensure that each specialized creative task is performed by the right person for the job. Perhaps it's why, after decades in business, Pentagram retains its place at the pinnacle of its industry, even as the industry has changed.[51]

The differences between Ken's company and Pentagram are stark. Although both companies are more than fifty years old, they have taken very different paths over the years, which has positioned them very differently. Where Ken's company puts products and services at the center, Pentagram puts people and ideas. That ingrained human-centric structure protects a forward-thinking culture at Pentagram. Even if biases and beliefs creep in, the operating culture helps to ensure they don't build up to the point of detriment.

While it's much harder for a company like Ken's to evolve, it's not impossible. Moreover, it is incredibly necessary. Defense and war are human endeavors. People are at the center of actions taken and of the outcomes of those actions. For Ken's company to serve its customers, it needs a deep understanding of how people execute the missions and tasks they are asked to accomplish to achieve national security goals.

Changing deep-rooted behaviors and beliefs takes a cultural shift that must happen locally, propelled and protected by human-centric-seeking leadership. Pushing new organizational constructs will challenge the status quo. It will elicit concern from those who take comfort in or haven't bothered to try to erase old paradigms. But courageous and committed human-centric leaders can set and nurture a fresh direction.

The catalyst for transformation will be to confront the reality of the challenge and aggressively pinpoint the hindrances to real change.

Thinking About Knowledge

With the rate of knowledge advancing exponentially every year, the expiration date of what we learn via education structures also gets shorter. With the ability to access learning anywhere and anytime, the need to capture and memorize facts becomes outmoded and unnecessary. At the TEDx-FoggyBottom, the Aramark CTO and chief AI officer Pavan Arora challenged an auditorium full of students to think differently about knowledge.[52] Arora's message focused on the need for lifelong learning. While his audience comprised students, his message is equally relevant to business leaders. He maintained that it's necessary to continually assess and reassess the sources and purpose of the information that we use to make decisions and do our work. He explained that as knowledge becomes more prevalent and commoditized, it alters our presumptions about what qualifies as critical understanding and learning.

Arora argued that the education system is not for teaching knowledge. Instead, it is to train people to become knowledge agnostic, creative, and capable problem-solvers. As the shelf life of knowledge shortens and the capacity for judgment becomes more important, people must know how to access information, assess its quality and usefulness, and use it to innovate or problem-solve.

Knowing *how* to use knowledge takes priority over *what* we need to learn. That means remembering that data is useful, but it is not truth. Truth requires context. It also means we absolutely have to build the capacity to identify obsoledge and the willingness to dispose of it when it is present.

Keeping in mind Arora's audience, we should begin by reimagining our education system. It's a meta exercise, but by identifying the obsoledge within such an institution, we can begin to understand how deeply entrenched certain ways of thinking have become. Currently, more than $3 trillion is spent annually supporting a global public education system that is for the most part outmoded and inappropriate. Roughly 1.5 billion people are currently being taught curriculum that hasn't significantly changed over the last hundred years.[53] Today's kindergarteners will graduate high school sometime after the year 2030, spend another two to four years (at minimum) in advanced education at a university or a trade school, and enter the workforce around the time of the 2040 U.S. presidential election. By then, they'll begin their careers or compete for jobs in a workplace and world that will be almost unrecognizable to what we know today.

As it stands, many of today's jobs are already on the verge of extinction. One estimate claims that 85 percent of jobs in 2030 haven't been created yet.[54] Advanced technology is replacing people in roles where it's necessary to perform menial tasks faster, cheaper, and more precisely. Hadi Partovi, CEO of the education nonprofit Code.org, challenges us to figure out the changes we need to make so the education system meets the workforce needs of the future. He advocates for teaching relevant curricula focused on how the world works, having children learn subjects like algorithms, robotics, machine learning, and artificial intelligence.[55] As software and the cloud continue to change every part of our world, basic computer science is needed for most jobs, whether that be in energy, health, manufacturing, or even professional services. And as technology becomes more capable, accurate, and fast at performing logical intelligence tasks such as machine learning and data analytics, human emotional intelligence and interpersonal and intrapersonal skills will become more important. These skills are required for organizations to understand human intentions, motivations, and desires and to act with diplomacy, courage, empathy, and enthusiasm for all stakeholders.

Shedding Organizational Blinders

As we look at the complex global marketplace, it is tempting for businesses to rely on data as the most reliable and ample source of information. At some point in the great knowledge grab, companies adopted a philosophy that "more data is better data." It took less than a decade to realize the problem with this assumption.

Free to operate with unlimited information, many organizations neglect to look collectively at inputs and assess what insights are most important to the future. As the Buckminster curve accelerates, it's become clear that more data does not always guarantee intelligent, well-made decisions. In fact, it creates a risk of the opposite if the organization isn't fine-tuned for the best possible purpose and future positioning.

For their book *Billion Dollar Failures: What You Can Learn from the Most Inexcusable Business Failures of the Last 25 Years,* Chunka Mui and Paul Carroll researched thousands of case

Deborah Westphal

studies to identify the 750 most significant collapses.[56] The number of failures Mui and Carroll profiled is staggering: 423 companies, each with assets of more than $500 million, filed for bankruptcy. The combined assets of these companies had exceeded $1.5 trillion. Yet some of these "too big to fail" companies had declared bankruptcy multiple times.

Their thesis was that most executives bristle at acknowledging their missteps, so their organizations rarely learn from past mistakes. Mui and Carroll found the most significant business downfalls were less likely to be the result of sloppy execution, poor leadership, or bad luck. Instead, most came from misguided strategies—in other words, a failure to challenge outmoded ideas and to keep the spectrum of stakeholders at the center of their focus.

Mui and Carroll spotlighted seven common strategic failure patterns. The typical red flag? Faulty decision-making in complex situations because of behavioral patterns and cognitive predispositions. Humans take comfort in homing in on presumed answers before examining all the facts, taking action, and seeking or creating confirmation. We do this even though we know intuitively that emotion, loyalties, and groupthink have outsized, often harmful impacts. We believe market behaviors will continue or evolve in predictable ways and act on those beliefs, even though we can't possibly know the future. We tend to avoid people or systems that challenge our assumptions, instead gravitating to those that support it, without really questioning either one.

Almost half the failures Mui and Carroll profiled could have been avoided if the companies had been more aware of pitfalls and willing to see warning signs. As they demonstrated, the perspective is outside the scope of ability for many organizations and leaders.

We began this book discussing why knowing humans is a priority for resilience. As businesses strive to keep pace with crosscurrents of disruption and progress, the thoughtful, human-centric approach offers a reliable formula for challenging the status quo, overcoming obsoledge, and expanding the knowledge aperture. In the end, the human-centric model positions us to adapt and respond appropriately because we can rely on people in the organization to help to separate noise from actual knowledge. When we do, the organization can tidy up, keep the clutter out, and progress with agility.

Moving toward the Future

Daring to envision a different version of the organization helps leaders analyze what is required in the present to put their people on the best path forward. Based on what we know about our contemporary reality, the ideal organization is human-centric, rather than process-driven and siloed. And we know that the challenge of getting to that ideal state starts with intentionally questioning deeply ingrained, status quo behaviors.

The "clean sheet" exercise is an excellent way for leaders to visualize the ideal organization and bring clarity to strategy-making and operational actions. It begins with two simple questions: If you could start with a clean sheet, would you create the same organization you have, or would you design it differently? If you wanted to design your corporation optimally for executing your concept of human-centric operations, what would it look like?[57] Done right, the activity can be a reliable first step in shedding the constraints of out-of-date structures, habits, assumptions, and biases.

Even with the possibility of a healthier future for the organization and the people in its ecosystem, the process can be tricky and uncomfortable for those who have to do the work. But orienting the business around its people and orienting its people around a common direction can help create forward momentum. Somewhat unexpectedly, we can find inspiration for this approach in the migratory behavior of birds.

Flocks of starlings coordinate themselves and move together with remarkable agility to find food and avoid attacks. The behavior is known as murmurations. The starlings' acrobatics combines speed and scale to create a synchronized movement for survival. The murmurations lack of an apparent leader. However, each bird knows and follows simple rules: align direction and speed, move apart if too close, and move closer if distance is too far from the flock. These shared rules enable each bird to act independently, even as they support the cohesion of the group.[58,59]

Human-centered organizations are like starling murmurations. They move in concert toward opportunity and away from endless sources of threat. Every member of the group is a valuable contributor. Together, they extend the organization's ability to observe, orient, decide, and act in agile unison. As they do, they strengthen their collective ability to pursue or create the future. Transforming from a striated, siloed organization to a human-centric model has the added benefit of cementing guiding core beliefs that inform shared decisions and behaviors. It also provides a reliable framework for eliminating obsoledge to make room for the most necessary knowledge.

From Conformity to Choice

All this sharing in the human-centric organization does not erase our individual need for personalization. Each of us holds unique preferences for everything from food to exercise to entertainment and more. Our work is no different. Members of the contemporary workforce are reluctant to be forced into a role, most seeking a profession that sharpens their skills, sparks their interests, and activates their reward centers. In other words, even as the value of the human-centric organization becomes ever more apparent, it's critical that we don't mistake it for a form of workforce conformity.

Efforts are under way to ensure the emerging workforce has choice in what they do. Higher education is being disrupted by trends toward micro-accreditation and micro-credentialing. This alternative approach to collegiate and postgraduate learning is rapidly renovating the professional pathway. These types of approaches are especially important for technical skills and knowledge. On average, half the knowledge learned in the first year of a technical four-year degree is obsolete by graduation.[60] New approaches to credentialing can help to bridge this chasm by engaging lifelong learners to develop new skills, but instituting them requires proactive thinking in the present to prepare for the future.

During the Industrial Revolution, the need to segment the organization into specific skill categories resulted in educational systems designed to institutionalize, reproduce, and validate particular occupations or career structures. As work and job positions became more specialized to support growing business objectives, the need to produce specific expertise also increased, maturing the higher education sector.

Customization and education for the sake of broad knowledge, rather than pure skill, have evolved into personalized learning structures. Professionals can train and reskill for different roles at different times for varied purposes, remaining *individually* relevant and fulfilled. For the organization, this flexibility is a way to actively support each person's uniqueness and create a nimble environment that keeps everyone capable and motivated to pursue shared goals.

Organizational and talent development are changing the nature of group and individualized work. So is the rapid and continuous adoption of advanced technologies like AI, autonomous technology, and robotics. While AI and ML may not be as essential as many leaders believe, the speed at which we are moving toward human-machine convergence demands we recognize that technology has a place on the team. It's this mix of willing and capable people, carefully employing intelligent technologies, that will allow the human-centric organization to understand, plan for, and adapt to the opportunity landscape. This construct is not one informed by old, industrial-era mental models.

From Silos to Spheres

With the evolving definition of *useful knowledge* and the proliferation of technology in the organization, logic has reigned as the most valuable form of intelligence. That honed capacity for math and science, pattern identification, and deductive reasoning are slowly but surely being balanced by more traditionally humanities-oriented soft skills.

For leaders striving to cultivate an organization capable of flexibility, collaboration, transdisciplinary thinking, and future-focus, it's intuitive, creative, emotional intellects that are needed to give logical skills purpose and place in the market. Creating a balanced portfolio of attributes, personalities and intelligences is key to achieving strategic, lasting success. In short, they help young leaders develop core values that sustain human-centric organizations.

We know for certain that valuing the full sphere of each person's capabilities and interests, instead of assigning them based on tactical skills, will increase innovation and competitiveness. That recognition and effort to put people at the center of the organization for the good of the business system and the human system it serves takes obsoledge head-on.

Obsoledge to Human-centric

We are operating in an unsettled, progressive age. Structures are fluid. Collaboration is boundless. New information emerges and joins the network daily, revealing new insights and ideas. It's a chaotic and incredibly exciting time to lead.

We've established that the law of obsoledge says that accelerating change creates new information and not all the inputs retain their usefulness. More knowledge means more obsoledge. The cycle is perpetual. How we choose to separate fact from belief can determine how confidently and quickly we can make decisions and proceed in the right direction.

By building a mental model that can filter this rising, free-flowing tide of inputs, we can harness their potential. This effort is not a task to do or a list to check. It is a continued awareness and willingness to identify and dispose of the beliefs, ideas, and behaviors that clutter our shared path to progress.

chapter six

Leadership Reboot

The leaders of tomorrow may well have to deal with a far more
decentralized and participatory society. . . . Leadership may well prove
to be more temporary, collegial, and consensual.

—Alvin Toffler, *The Third Wave* (1980)

The early hours of February 13, 2019, marked an important
personal milestone. I had made it to the summit of Mount
Kilimanjaro. At an elevation of 19,341 feet, Mount Kilimanjaro
is one of the elite Seven Summits—the highest mountains
on each of the seven continents. Every year, approximately thirty-five thousand people attempt the summit. Only
about two-thirds succeed. While the climb does not require
special mountaineering equipment, all the trekking routes
are strenuous, and problems related to altitude keep many
climbers from reaching the top.

My chosen journey was the Machame Route. It is a six-day
trek through five major ecological zones across rugged and
sometimes very steep sections and rock scramblings. I'm still
not sure what compelled me to hike Mount Kilimanjaro. I
most certainly am not an experienced hiker, but there I was.

As the sun began to rise the fifth morning, I stood atop
the highest mountain in Africa and the tallest freestanding
mountain in the world. My guide was Dismass Mariki, a local
Tanzanian who had made the journey to the summit of Kili
more than two hundred times.

The day before we began our trek up Mount Kilimanjaro,
Dismass took my seven trekking companions and me to the

Arusha National Park for an easy hike. He told us the activity would be a chance to shake out our equipment and begin the process of acclimation. We hiked almost five hours that day, and as we did so, Dismass was carefully and quietly observing us. He was assessing our skill, strengths, comfort with hiking and our equipment, and (most likely) weaknesses. After we returned from our hike that day, he conducted individual gear checks to ensure we each had what we needed for the trip. In hindsight, I'm sure he was making necessary adjustments to the trek plan based on our group's collective capability.

Dismass knew the pitfalls and hazards of the journey. As we made our way up the mountain, he would calmly deflect our questions to a more appropriate time by telling us he would make sure we knew everything we needed to know when we needed to know it. At night, during dinner, he would share his wisdom by telling us stories of past treks and experiences with others. Inside each of these stories was an important message—if we listened, we would be prepared for the next day and the challenges we would face.

Dismass hasn't gone to business school. He hasn't been to formal leadership training. Books and podcasts on leadership are not resources he consumes. He doesn't have a title or employees to manage. And yet there is no question that Dismass is a leader. He showed courage and determination in his responsibility to get our group to the summit and back safely. In only a matter of days, his actions inspired deep trust, followership, and respect. He made himself available to get the best out of us. This humble gesture was a living reminder of real leadership.

As a concept, leadership is both incredibly powerful and incredibly damaged by overuse. People apply the term to a diverse range of actions, attributes, behaviors, and positions.

Do a quick search on Amazon (in 2020), and you'll find more than ninety thousand books in the category. There are millions of scholarly and journalistic articles written on the subject. All that chatter might make leadership seem complicated.

It isn't.

Leadership is the fundamental ability to behave with humility and wisdom, to engage authentically, and to inspire others toward achieving a purpose they might never accomplish on their own. This definition isn't necessarily how we've historically thought about leadership. Between the late 1700s and the end of the 1800s, the prevailing leadership philosophies embraced the great man and trait theories, which proposed that certain men are *born* to lead. Successful leaders stood on platforms of consistency, standardization, compliance, reporting, efficiency, and performance.

That thinking generally held until the 1950s, when emerging behavioral theory attempted to describe leadership based on what leaders *do*, rather than leaning on who they *are*. The concept focused on critical behavioral determinants that could be used to train people to become leaders. Both trait and behavioral theories illustrated leadership through the lens of the individual but neglected two critical components that we now know to be vital: the leader's environment and the quality of his or her subordinates.

Dr. Paul Hersey and Dr. Ken Blanchard introduced the situational leadership theory, which suggested that leaders choose a leadership style based on the developmental maturity of their team members.[61] So much of what we have learned about leadership focuses on what we do and how we do it. Dismass proved the value of the situational leadership theory. Others like Andrés, Fink, and Price have as well. As we look closer to spot human-centric behaviors, we see the old guard model of business leadership evolving toward this more courageous, personal model. Openness replaces ego. Trust and creativity hold priority over policy and process. Culture and cognitive diversity take precedence over strict adherence to form and function. We can feel real empathy in the decisions and actions of others.

These leaders invite others to share human connections to achieve something greater than any one person. The most notable are valued not only for their experience and persona but also for their courage. They recognize and share themselves honestly, deeply, and sincerely. And they inspire the same in others. They are aware of their role in the human system, and because they are, they act with authenticity and humility. Through these individuals, we are witnessing the shift to human-centric leadership, from shareholder to stakeholder, and from top-down to genuinely relational.

With this new lens in place, it's no longer enough for leadership to define itself by how it sets strategic direction, defines performance goals, aligns functions and processes, and manages performance. Even as these functions remain essential, they are second to the soft skills of our best leaders—skills like honesty, personal reflection, and humility. In other words, the value of a human-centric leader is as much about *who* they are as what they *do*.

Human-centric Leadership

For the last several decades, most prominent organizations have captured dominance by innovating faster and with more agility than the competition and by sustaining market relevance and producing shareholder return. Turning the focus to meeting the needs of a broader spectrum of stakeholders will require putting people, not products or balance sheets, at the center of the organizational strategy.

Transitioning to a human-centric perspective has a higher probability of positive impact over the long term on profitability, growth, and performance, and not just for shareholders. While many are measurable with mathematical benchmarks, not all these positive outcomes are metrics based. Countless case studies (like Gravity Payments) show that businesses and the people in them are more likely to succeed in the face of challenge and capture more opportunities for the future if they are bound and guided by a shared set of beliefs, decisions, and actions.

It's the job of the human-centric leader to keep those priorities in order and to be the first to break down old, outmoded paradigms. The new purpose of business centers on stakeholders—all those people who are a part of the concentric circles of relationships that move outward from the organization.

Leaders need to listen and respond to concerns from stakeholders outside the organization about issues like climate change or animal cruelty with responsible manufacturing processes. Inside the organization, leaders need to inspire and equip a group of people (who may expect their primary role is to earn their paycheck) to contribute knowledge, skills, energy, experiences, vulnerability, and drive to help the group accomplish extraordinary things. In both cases, being human-centric and focused on stakeholders requires courage and the commitment to change behaviors to unleash positive human energy.

Most of our long-held beliefs about leaders have more to do with what they *do* than who they *are*. Although modern perspectives have progressed beyond the idea that leadership is a destiny, a particular mythos remains. But we can't lose sight of the fact that every organization is a collection of humans, whether that organization is a two-person start-up or an enterprise of international scale.

Leadership orients and motivates people in the same direction and supports them along the path to purpose, especially when the journey becomes difficult. Motivation and support are human endeavors. They are not tasks to be delegated. Others can help you to push them forward, but the responsibility is yours to own.

An Honest Look Inside

Most of us who strive to be efficient, productive leaders try to learn from our professional experiences. We study and read. We have conversations. We experiment and get feedback. We compare and contrast our actions to others' conduct. We make interpretations and comparisons to draw conclusions about our strengths, weaknesses, behaviors, and capacity. Then we bake the beliefs into a persona. With all that collecting, we rarely take the time to clarify the errors and misinformation that no longer serve our purpose. We rarely take the time to truly self-reflect on our values, beliefs, biases, and behaviors.

Self-awareness is an exceptional leadership skill. It takes courage and vulnerability to achieve, neither of which is comfortable or easy. Often those skills are discovered and honed during times of uncertainty, risk, and emotional exposure. They are proven out by doing the hard work to show up, be fully engaged, and take responsibility before knowing the outcome. Even the personal practice of mindfulness can nurture increased leadership self-awareness.

On a wall in the Brighton Resort ski lodge, located outside of Salt Lake City, Utah, there is a tiny plaque that simply states "BE." For years, I would go skiing at Brighton and wonder what "BE" meant. It seemed like an odd statement. What was its importance? What was I missing? What am I supposed to "BE"?

It wasn't until after being introduced to Dr. Brené Brown's work did I finally understand the meaning of "BE"—*be* present, *be* vulnerable, *be* authentic. *Be* human. *Be* mindful. That drive to *be* has begun to infiltrate business—a world shaped by process, standards, and hard numbers. Being mindful is a mental state achieved by focusing one's awareness on the present moment, while calmly acknowledging and accepting one's feelings, thoughts, and bodily sensations.

Most leaders are readers, so there's a chance you've come across headlines like "How Meditation Benefits CEOs," "Does Mindfulness Training Have Business Benefits?," "Tech Addiction and the Business of Mindfulness," and "Mindfulness as Leadership Practice" in your daily readings. Though promoted as tools to cope with stress and the rapid pace of our changing society, improve focus and productivity, and even make people better leaders, these are not new concepts. On the contrary, meditation and mindfulness have deep roots in Hindu and Buddhist traditions, lending even more credence to the fact that the true definition of a leader is not based on a title or role; rather it is based on behavior.

A side benefit of a deliberate practice of self-awareness is a greater sense of our place in the human system; it can illuminate how our individual interests as humans cannot simply be categorized into neat boxes for easy problem-solving. For leaders, embracing the reality that most situations and circumstances are outside the range of our control is a fundamental step in being capable of leading a human-centric organization toward positive exponential change. As Brown writes, "...true belonging only happens when we present our authentic, imperfect selves to the world, our sense of belonging can never be greater than our level of self-acceptance.[62]

Most of today's "mature" leaders did not grow up believing in the value of vulnerability. Quite the opposite. Those of us who launched our careers during the later part of the twentieth century learned to fear that unfiltered state as a sign of weakness. We earned positions in corporations that built hierarchies to organize people by task and skill with the sole intent of delivering specific, measurable outcomes. For those who cut their teeth as executives in such structures, the approach feels more controlled and comfortable. The problem is that these organizational charts and authoritarian leadership approaches don't work in human-centric organizations. Leaders have moved from the top of the ladder to the center of the organization. Leadership is horizontal, networked, and relational instead of top-down and dictatorial.

We also got used to shutting off emotions in the workplace. (Perhaps that's why it took me so long to understand the value of *be*.) Integrating AI into the workforce could exacerbate that problem—or we could allow the machines to create the space for us to engage with others, ask deeper "why" questions, consider what we reason to be true, and truly understand that the value we bring to our business is our humanness.

A new leadership style has begun to emerge from this move to cultivate a deep understanding of *who* we are as individuals. Knowing how we make decisions and why we make them the way we do is critical. Recognizing our individual biases and belief systems is foundational. Nurturing the ability to determine when these parts of ourselves get in the way of our capacity to lead from a place of transparency is required. Creating personal routines that search for obsoledge within our own decision-making systems will open up new opportunities for learning and personal growth.

In a rapidly changing and disruptive time, the stakes are incredibly high for those who want to lead with authenticity. As technology and human systems converge, they fight for attention and power, making the markets noisier and more confusing. It's getting harder to distinguish between what information can be believed and what might be fake, altered, or manipulated. For those who feel compelled to address every news item, comment, and criticism they receive, knowing what needs their attention and what can or should be ignored is getting harder.

Yesterday's means of communicating with the market are obfuscating the intended context of our operations and decision-making. To gain trust going forward, we must find new ways of connecting with those who are important to our companies' success. This task of building trust is one requirement of authentic leadership. So is the need to be transparent with our actions and the actions of the organizations we lead. But even if we do attempt to build trust and transparency, proving why we should be trusted is now also a part of the equation.

No longer can we deflect blame for a poorly received message or initiative to unintended procedures or the larger operating system. The market won't tolerate it. Ironically, the more complex and interconnected everything becomes, the less we can hide our actions and decisions. As leaders of human-centric organizations, believability begins with knowing ourselves and holding fast to the courage to remain consistent to our values. Consistent authenticity may be the only panacea to a world of noise and confusion.

chapter seven
Truth, Transparency, and Trust

Even if we set aside "obsoledge"—obsolete knowledge—how much of
what we know about money, business and wealth—or anything else—
is total nonsense? Or pure fiction? How much can we trust what we're
being told? How do we decide? And even more important, who
decides how we decide?

—Alvin and Heidi Toffler, *Revolutionary Wealth* (2006)

By now we have all heard of the rise and fall of Theranos, a
company that set out to revolutionize blood testing—and the
health-care industry—by drastically decreasing the amounts
of blood that needed to be drawn and using automation for
near real-time results. With Theranos, a future with at-home
testing and personalized health-care maintenance was nearly
in sight.

Thanks in no small part to Netflix, most of us also know the
young, energetic, and charismatic CEO of Theranos, Elizabeth Holmes, who was just nineteen when she dropped out
of Stanford University in 2003 to form her start-up. Tireless
in her pursuit of supporters, especially investors, she told
and retold her story of personal loss, which she indicated
was a driving purpose for the creation of Theranos. She
would describe how applying advanced technology to human
needs would help millions of people and save lives. From
the beginning it was clear that Holmes was seeking the
mantle of "disrupter" to the $70 billion U.S. diagnostic-lab
industry.

Notable financial backers started to take interest. Holmes
raised more than $700 million from high-profile investors,

and her board consisted of powerhouse players like Henry Kissinger, George Shultz, former secretaries of defense, U.S. senators, and even William Foege, former director of the Centers for Disease Control and Prevention. By 2014, Theranos was valued at an estimated $9 billion.

Holmes became the world's youngest female self-made billionaire. The media loved her: the *Wall Street Journal* praised Holmes repeatedly and *Fortune* put her on the cover. The accolades were wide: *Forbes* named her one of the richest self-made women in the world and *Time* selected her as one of its one hundred most influential people.[63] Numerous articles and interviews promulgated her story of pursuit, passion, and success.

And then in 2018, as we all know, the tables turned for Holmes. The Securities and Exchange Commission charged Theranos, Holmes, and Ramesh Balwani, Theranos's former president, with raising more than $700 million from investors through an elaborate, years-long fraud in which they exaggerated or made false statements about the company's technology, business, and financial performance.[64] Holmes and Balwani deceived investors into believing that the Theranos portable blood analyzer worked. In truth, Theranos had conducted the vast majority of patient tests on modified and industry-standard commercial analyzers manufactured by others. Performance data about the company's progress was based on a foundation of obfuscation and untruths.

Holmes's story was widely shared in detail. People were both shocked and fascinated by her behavior. The truth of the story, however, is less interesting than what it represents. In many ways, Holmes is simply an old-fashioned snake oil salesperson. While this type of behavior is nothing new, it is an example of how a person positioned as an authority can have widespread impact on our lives, especially in our highly connected world. She manipulated very smart and experienced investors by hijacking reasoning by triggering emotion. Holmes exploited the emotional vulnerabilities of her investors, using their commitment to her idea to create a shield of legitimacy. With this, she was able to undermine and devalue transparency within Theranos to the point of nonexistence. She gave false hope to those desperate for the science to save lives.

While Holmes's intentions to influence were criminal, others may use similar emotional techniques for non-nefarious pursuits. The problem is, when some people are using the methods for deceit and others are using them for good, it takes work to know the true motive or purpose of those we are supposed to trust before it's too late. And it is only going to get harder to know what and whom to trust. Technology for deception, deep fakes, and the manipulation of what we see and hear is advancing at the speed of heat. Holmes's story is a warning of how easy it is to manipulate through emotional vulnerabilities and use technology to expand reach.

Given the extensive knowledge available in today's info-sphere, it can be overwhelming and frustrating to spot authority and know if it can be trusted. Those people traditionally held accountable for aggregating information, breaking news, and presenting it to the public still position themselves as trust-worthy. But accepting information as presented is getting harder to do, making context and transparency even more essential. Leaders must understand these new dynamics. Without it we can't build trust.

Crisis in Trust

The concept of trust gets a lot of airtime. A scroll through your media feed will inevitably land you in the midst of an ongoing debate over our trust in media, government, business, and one another. For the past twenty years, the global communications firm Edelman has been researching trust, and it is not surprising that its studies show deep shifts in public sentiment. Edelman's *2020 Trust Barometer* report reveals just how uncertain many people feel about institutions, including businesses.[65]

What is certain and enduring is that trust is a make-or-break proposition. People *want* businesses to act on issues including wage inequality, the environment, and social injustice—but don't actually *believe* they will. The *2020 Trust Barometer* points out that ethical drivers are three times more important to trusting a company than its competence, including its purpose, ability, and dependability. And respondents say they feel like current business structures are failing them.

The Pew Research Center confirms we're experiencing a crisis in trust.[66] A highly detailed study from 2019 drilled down into the erosion of our confidence levels. Scientists and the military sit at the top of the trust pile, with more than 80 percent of Americans reporting a fair amount of confidence in these groups to act in the best interests of the public. Our religious leaders, college and university professors, and (interestingly) journalists sit in the middle of the pack. Elected officials and business leaders are at the bottom. More than 40 percent of the survey group report having little confidence or trust in business leaders; 14 percent say they have none.

Sandra J. Sucher and Shalene Gupta, in their *Harvard Business Review* piece on trust in modern institutions, "The Trust Crisis," point out the financial consequences of corporate betrayals.[67] In 2018, eight of the largest business scandals diminished the value of each respective company by 30 percent of its original projected worth. Sucher and Gupta argue that building strong relationships with stakeholders demands more than good public relations. Creating and sustaining trust requires clear purpose, aligned strategy, and definitive action to acknowledge and remediate negative decisions when necessary.

We decide whether to project trustworthiness on a daily basis. It happens in thousands of routine interactions with stakeholders. We build trust by consistently delivering on promises and going to great lengths to rectify the situation when we fail to deliver. When we behave in ways that show that we prioritize being able to satisfy each stakeholder's needs and well-being, we communicate that our business is human-centric. And when we do that, there is a high probability that trust can be built between our business system and the human system.

Omniscience

Name an organization that is not somehow connected to the internet. In our hyperconnected global economy that's a near-impossible task. One of the main reasons businesses have put so much stock into building connectivity is because it generates the virtual presence they need to gain the confidence of customers, suppliers, and the communities they serve. In turn, customers often provide businesses with their own data—a valuable commodity that now lives at the epicenter of our trust crisis.

Data flows beneath and through every organization, industry, society, and economy, like the currents that shape the Galápagos. Billions of sensors are embedded in almost every product, machinery, and structure. Growing numbers of advanced sensors track our behaviors and preferences— the patterns of human life. They collect and distribute data across massive networks, creating new information and insights about the world. It is a gigantic system, fed constantly by human behavior, interfacing throughout the system of systems.

Experts working to forecast the worldwide growth of data traffic employ numeric terms like *zettabytes* (10^{21}) and *yottabytes* (10^{24}).[68] The measures represent the enormous amounts of data that exist for businesses to wrangle and exploit. Most of us struggle to wrap our minds around the magnitude of a zettabyte or yottabyte. We can, however, grasp the idea that our access to and reliance on data has thrust us into a new era for business.

There's no doubt that data is a powerful tool for today's leaders. It can empower us to improve our internal operational practices to be more efficient and effective. It can give us unique insight into our customers. And it can be a competitive edge and a position of authority. If there's any doubt that business decisions must be data-driven, just do a cursory Google search using words like *data* or *data-driven decisions*. Within seconds, the search will yield thousands of articles, podcasts, and other content about the importance of data for business.

Besides the academic exercises, you'll also find promises that data-driven decisions will make businesses less vulnerable. Breathless, almost panicky make-or-break assertions move leaders to strive to adopt data-driven practices. The world's largest strategy consulting firms support these perspectives. In recent years, they have expanded their offerings to help customers link business strategy with technology strategy. New digital strategy lines seem to have cropped up everywhere. McKinsey & Company has observed that 40 percent of its work falls within the McKinsey Digital umbrella.[69] As influential companies focus on scaling technology across enterprises to move faster, adapt to market needs, and increase business performance and outcomes, they are feeding the momentum of technology.

If organizations design digital strategies that use technology to improve performance optimized only for shareholders, they run the risk of those priorities permeating overall decision- making. Unfortunately, algorithms are not nearly as sophisticated as humans when it comes to considering the broader and far more nuanced spectrum of stakeholders for a given business. The strange result is that new, cutting-edge technology strategies often bake in old models and yesterday's business practices, leaving little room to integrate broader perspectives such as environmental or social issues. In effect, there is a lot more data, but it is often simply doing more of the same old thing.

More Data, Better Context

In an interview with *Forbes*, Sara Spivey, the chief marketing officer of cloud-based software company Braze, described the "more data is better data" problem.[70] Not so long ago, companies were forced to operate with limited information. In an effort to glean any useful insights, they needed to look collectively at all their inputs. As that information proliferated (rapidly), they had more information to use, but not all of it was useful. We arrived at the new issue of knowing what insights to trust.

Clarifying the problem, identifying outmoded or inappropriate concepts and ideas, and accurately interpreting the body of information help to fuel intelligent business decisions with lasting positive implications. The logic-based process engages the *criticality of context* to find fact and eliminate interpretation bias. Without true data to anchor knowledge, past beliefs and out-of-date processes threaten the usefulness of the decisions.

We know this. So why do so many organizations prioritize building robust stores of information, rather than working to institute processes that ensure the data is contextually valuable?

Perhaps it's because we are generally comfortable with the idea that *data is truth*. Among those who are tasked with acquiring and analyzing the vast oceans of inputs that power modern society, this belief is spreading rapidly. We want to conclude that if we have enough of the right data, we can spot the truth in it. These beliefs must come with a caveat. Data gives us numbers. *Context* situates it within value, importance, and reason. It informs our assumptions about the relationships between data and the environment around us. It helps us to determine the appropriate metrics to use to gauge the quality of our information and the uniqueness, categorization, and importance of our insights.

This is not to say that numbers are unimportant. They are. We manage our lives with numbers. For example, we use smartwatches or Fitbits to track how many steps we take each day. We use these same devices to track how much sleep we get at night. We count calories consumed, calories burned, minutes we meditate, and time we spend flipping through social media. We use numbers to segment our day into smaller and smaller chunks of time. But it is the *context* of these numbers that hold meaning. The context tells us if we are doing what's necessary to improve our health and ward off illness or disease. So answering the question of whether five thousand steps are good, bad, or neutral depends on who is taking the steps, their relative condition, and the kind of environment in which these steps are being taken.

In a world of near-infinite inputs, organizations must be able to confirm that they can rely on the validity of their insights. One fundamental question in this balancing act is whether, given inherent bias, we can trust our own data.

Even with AI and ML doing much of the heavy lifting in the modeling and analysis process, for example, human bias can still represent a fatal flaw in the system. We need to employ reliable mental models that can confirm the transparency of intent and the validity and trustworthiness of the information. We also need an ontology to organize the outputs into targeted, objective answers.

We use personal experiences with data and our own truths to assign value to numbers. It's why contextual awareness is critical. The consequences of our data-based decisions can impact and disrupt other decisions, activities, even lives. Context brings humanness to data by guiding what decisions we need to make, why we are making those decisions, and whom we are making them for. This human perspective of the data can provide much-needed transparency and trust with stakeholders.

And it's that transparency we require for trust to exist between those making decisions and those on the receiving end of a decision made.

Momentum toward Divergence

Technology is the physical connector and people are the emotional connector. As such, humans bring energy and emotional electricity to build trusting relationships. And while it makes sense that ever-evolving technology unleashes the energy we see throughout the human system, it is short-sighted to ignore the fact that humans, not technology, build trust within an organization.

Humanness is needed for our organizations to build trust with all the people we engage and serve inside and outside the organization. Following technology's drumbeat will only widen the chasm between where we are and the human-centric state we need to reach. Trusted relationships are the vector for knowledge transfer. The more trusted relationships are developed and proactively managed, the more knowledge we can transfer.

The IBM Institute for Business Value has posited that humanity has entered the insights era, a phase in which the full potential of data can be realized.[71] The advent of AI, the internet of things, and cloud computing have given us the means to turn "bytes into insights" and generate contextualized, predictive knowledge. This is a technology-centric assessment of the power of data and insights, limited in its view of how they connect the power shift to humanity.

I would argue that we have been operating in the insights era for quite a while and that it's broader than IBM describes. We need to see this phase as more than a forum for innovating and marketing emerging technologies that can produce hard information to fuel ideas and decisions. We need to put our focus on the ideas and decisions themselves and then consider the technology and data as the tools. Reversing this priority order creates space to contextualize knowledge and decisions within ethics, character, and shared morals. It elevates the importance of the insights, as well as the context and data we're using to inform them.

Humans are cognizant of the many benefits of technology. The question is how businesses can and should use technology, data, and insights to pursue solutions for the issues burdening societies, economies, and individuals. We know that most organizations are collecting and analyzing enormous amounts of data. We hear corporate messages about caring for customers, communities, and humanity. Yet we remain unsure about whether we should trust those commitments.

It's not surprising. Technology has created a revolutionary wealth system where human experiences provide corporations with free raw materials for economic gain. While technology is improving the human condition, there is clear evidence that collection, prediction, and sales cycles can lead to manipulation of customers and possibly even behavior modification.

Media is a perfect example of this complex challenge. Though it's often viewed and defined as a single entity ("the media"), it is not. Adding to the confusion, some people use *media* as a derogatory term to describe the behavior of being duped or misled. In reality, media channels are businesses, each with its own goals. They both consume vast amounts of data and market vast amounts of ideas and information. Together, individuals and companies need to become more accountable for how data is interpreted and used.

Shoshana Zuboff challenges the proclamation that businesses act in good faith when it comes to the data they collect from humanity. She is not alone in her concern. The question is how business leaders can prioritize transparency and trust. A good start is to promote the context of our decisions. That transparency will help employees, customers, and the broader marketplace understand why things are being done the way they are. It may be the only way to grow the foundation of trust that is required in the Knowledge Age.

A Timeline to the Present

We can trace the systematic practice of developing technology specifically to improve business operations back to around the early 1900s. It was the industrial era, and mass production manufacturing was taking hold and growing rapidly. Manufacturing plants were challenged to rethink their processes in order to meet the accelerating market demand for products and goods. With customers like the military demanding bulk quantities, manufacturing companies set up assembly lines to optimize the flow of production output.

During this same time, the first mainframe computing capability was being developed. These new computers could crunch data faster, helping decision-makers see where they could make improvements in performance. Companies were using technology to collect and analyze their own data for their own use. It was an internal effort performed for the benefit of the company itself. There was little incentive to manipulate the data for the benefit of others. It was as trustworthy as it could be, given the newness of the technology.

A fundamental shift in how businesses used data happened sometime around the 1980s. Computing power increased, computers shrunk to fit on desktops, and networking technology was taking off. Through 2015, organizations began to shift their technology investments externally, toward the market.

Business was globalizing. The need to manage a magnitude of complex relationships grew. With opportunities to serve new global markets, technology became a vital tool to understand market dynamics and customer behaviors. Business intelligence became a thing. Companies raced to invest in network computing and data processing to create the capability to align what was happening inside organizations to what was happening outside. They began to obscure collection techniques as business intelligence grew into a competitive advantage. Data and insights were assets to protect. And the doubts about trustworthiness grew.

As the technology evolved, so did our business structures and leadership roles. Each period of change brought new opportunities for new types of leaders to wield influence. It wasn't easy. Leaders in every era have wrestled to understand change and spot the right priorities, decision-making models, and actions to achieve successful transformation. As the urgency of these evolutions and decisions has accelerated, so have the notions of transparency and trust.

The Rise of the Roles

As our use of technology evolved, so did the need for someone to lead it. In the 1980s, the chief information officer (CIO) held considerable influence over the strategic direction of an organization, determining which technologies to implement to ensure a leaner, faster, more process-compliant organization. CIOs were internal change agents responsible for transforming their companies to reduce clerical loads and improve transaction processing across enterprises. They achieved business relevance and influence by developing technology capability to translate strategy into execution. Their efforts to connect efforts happening within the company facilitated transparent internal decision-making and helped to build a culture of trust.

The dot-com boom of the late 1990s ushered in the role of the chief technology officer (CTO). CIOs had gotten bogged down with trying to keep processes running efficiently using the legacy systems they had in place. Information technology department strategies had outgrown their ability to maximize returns on investments. Attention turned to how technology could be used externally for business growth. The CTO took on the task of targeting improvements or even total overhauls of product or service offerings. It's at this point when we see the early stages of data-driven decision-making. Financial outcomes asserted the quality of technology investments. Transparency about technology projects, budgets, and impacts was necessary.

Customer data was shaping product line strategies. Companies gathered and analyzed information from the human system to create functions like customer experience, designed to improve engagement and sales. These functions were new competitive assets. It wasn't long before chief marketing officers (CMOs) became the darling of the C-suite. Their primary responsibility was monetizing the new technologies, products, and services developed by the CTO. The advances in data analytics, data science, automation, and customer relationship management had created a solid foundation from which the CMO could lead.

Recent advancements have moved content marketing and content strategy forward. Companies are producing all forms of content to stimulate attention, interest, and engagement with their products and services. They're pulling reams of data about how people respond and how it drives reputation, competitive positioning, sales, and more.

To be sure, companies will continue to invest in technology and efforts to reach and serve their teams, customers, and communities. They advertise these commitments. But if what they actually show through action is that the main purpose of their businesses is to only grow shareholder gains, their behaviors are misaligned with their promises. People will feel the lack of transparency and respond with distrust.

We are also "rearranging the deck chairs" across our organizational charts in an effort to determine the best roles to meet future needs. Especially as data flows through functions and performance metrics, it's not surprising to see organizations working to consolidate marketing, sales, product development, communications, and culture roles. The question remains whether we will measure the success of these new roles based on financial accountability or a higher level of intent, like the one Fink outlines in his shareholder letter. Will these new responsibilities satisfy the commitments that almost two hundred CEOs declared when they signed the "Statement on the Purpose of a Corporation"?

Organizations that hold tight to shareholder primacy also will hold themselves back from achieving the identity they proclaim to have and the position they want to capture. We must converge on the idea of transparency and trust to fulfill the desired outcomes for our businesses. Transparency about how our context frames our data creates the mechanism for trust to exist. And trust transforms words into relationships and actions.

No matter what purpose we proclaim, our behaviors reveal whether we still believe the primary purpose of our business is to serve shareholders. Changing decisions and behaviors requires that we see how we continue to concentrate on that primacy. Earning trust is not an issue we can solve with titles and responsibilities. People demand transparency and truth, and the future success of the organization depends on how well we earn trust by satisfying those demands. Those leaders who embrace transparency and produce content as evidence are well positioned to build trust.

And it's going to get much harder for us to build trust.

When you look at an image or video online, can you tell if it's been manipulated or not? And if you could, would it alter your opinion of it?[72] Advancing technologies are making it harder to recognize manipulations and deceit. It is getting difficult to trust what we hear and see.

The manipulation of pictures has a history almost as long as photography. The first known doctoring of a photograph was during the 1860 presidential campaign. Abraham Lincoln's opponents attacked Lincoln's looks, spreading rumors of his being ugly. They even went so far as to suggest that his appearance had something to do with his intellect. Given that photography was yet to be in widespread use or dissemination, most people had not seen what Lincoln actually looked like; they had only written descriptions in newspapers to inform their thoughts about Lincoln's ability to lead as president.

Lincoln, concerned about the impact of the media chatter, asked Mathew Brady, a well-known photographer at the time, to create an image to counter the negative press. Just before Lincoln's Cooper Union address, which would secure his nomination as the Republican candidate, Brady took his picture. Brady also did some photo touch-ups to smooth out Lincoln's sharp facial features and hide his long, thin neck. The picture became the first widely disseminated photo of a future president. It is rumored that Lincoln believed it helped him get elected president.

We have become entirely comfortable with manipulated pictures being used in advertising, entertainment, and social media. We know that Oprah Winfrey's head was placed on Ann-Margret's body for a 1989 cover of *TV Guide*, delight in the film work in *Forrest Gump*, and use apps on our phones to edit pictures before we post them. Even if these examples are innocuous, the danger isn't in the individual examples; it is in their intent.

A growing concern about advanced technologies, including AI, is their potential to be used nefariously. Recently, a senior executive of a UK-based energy firm thought he was speaking on the phone with his boss, who asked him to send almost a quarter million dollars to a Hungarian supplier. The request was urgent and had to be done immediately. What the senior executive didn't know was that while he recognized the voice on the other end of the line, the person talking wasn't someone he knew or authorized to make such a request.[73] This deep fake request was criminal.

While these examples are somewhat simplistic, they illustrate a growing problem for today's leaders. The ways and means to manipulate truths are raising in volume and power. Human-centric organizations must implement methodologies to ensure that the information used to make decisions is real. Taking on this task requires finding new ways to be transparent and counter the growing use of deep fakes to severely damage our companies. We mustn't allow the divergence of technology and humanity to feed into the momentum of this dangerous force. Positioning for truth and trust in a world where "alternative truths" compete for the trust of our stakeholders will mean new responsibilities for vigilance across our organizations.

Truth Filters

Perhaps the capabilities we need aren't new. Philosophers have debated the concept of truth for centuries. It's likely they will continue to do so for centuries to come. While the various perspectives are interesting, most are not as formative as the several filters most of us use to decide what is true. Our criteria often come from conventional wisdom or a decision to believe that if everyone believes X is true, it must be true.

Largely thanks to the speed and volume of social media distribution, consensus views form at lightning speed, often without much consideration or validation. We accept information delivered by people who claim authority and expertise. But with such fierce competition for share of voice and attention, real authority is rarely immediately clear.

The result of this cacophony is that it's almost impossible to separate truth from non-truth by looking at a single source or piece of information. For consumers, this reality means that knowing what to trust requires careful research and discernment. For businesses and leaders, it means trying to control messages that, once in the world, are about as manageable as a wildfire.

The influential political philosopher Hannah Arendt made a distinction between truth and meaning, saying, "The need of reason is not inspired by the quest for truth but by the quest for meaning."[74] This distinction between truth and meaning is especially important as we consider the massive investments made by companies to create and control the influence of information. Human-centric leaders are using technology investments to understand what constitutes the meaning, based on the premise that this data will give them a better understanding of their stakeholders and a clearer path to earning trust.

We must declare, actively embrace, and strategically pursue a new purpose of business. Once we do, we can modify or create the functions necessary to implement the strategies and to convey transparency and truth. Regardless of what those efforts entail, the end goal must be the authentic trust that comes from human connection. We must be conscious of the multidimensionality of the technology we are using. Others are using that technology too, some in ways that could be detrimental to our business goals and achievement.

We must advocate for and build truth filters capable of creating and sustaining trust. These filters must ensure the context of data and decisions are transparent. This means openly sharing what we know for certain and what we don't. Our intent must be clear and consistent, not obfuscated by conflicting intent. Only then can we rewire organizational charts and create new roles with accountability goals. The convergence of technology and humanity will most definitely shift the relationships between truth, transparency, and trust.

chapter eight
Tectonic Shifts

A new civilization is emerging in our lives, and blind men everywhere are trying to suppress it. This new civilization brings with it new family styles; changed ways of working, loving, and living; a new economy; new political conflicts; and beyond all this an altered consciousness as well.

—Alvin and Heidi Toffler, *Creating a New Civilization* (1994)

An old decade ends and a new one begins. Granted, these are arbitrary markers of relative time, but there is something momentous about the passage from one decade to the next. Whether it's with nostalgia or relief, we feel a sense of accomplishment for making it to the end of another ten-year stretch. Around the world, celebratory fireworks seem bigger and last longer. Social media chatter about hope for the new year and the decade ahead seems more robust and plentiful. Well-wishes for the future are shared more broadly. And, of course, we look back on the previous ten years and package it up into a story we can tell ourselves.

We felt this sense of significance at the end of 2019. The world was once again reflecting on the past decade, and humanity was full of anticipation to open a new chapter of history. Many of us reminisced about the past year—and the last decade. The events, experiences, accomplishments, even disappointments that we posted and described said a lot about our individual preferences and priorities.

For me, there were some real highlights. Traveling across Nepal, Bhutan, and Tibet for more than a month was soul shifting. Spending time in Croatia with my son, exploring the ancient cities of Split and Dubrovnik and eating watermelon gelato every day, gave us the gift of togetherness. Finishing my second Chicago marathon along with my running partner and forty thousand people from all over the world was an affirmation that age is just a number. Being one of the almost two million people who saw Pink perform live during her Beautiful Trauma tour reconnected me to the power of music and its community.

Billions of us traveled and explored locally and globally. We went to movies, concerts, and sporting events. We sent our children to school, attended church, celebrated holidays with friends and families. We went to work, some meandering on foot to an office down the street and others commuting long hours across the city in trains, cars, and buses. We planned, saved, spent, moved, gathered, celebrated, mourned, and lived. The human system moved, interacted, shared, hoped, dreamed, feared—and connected.

And then, at the very start of 2020, even as some of us were still reflecting on an eventful year, an "unforeseen consequence" (to use a gross understatement) of our connected humanity arose. An unknown and seemingly unstoppable pandemic began to sweep through the world. Government leaders turned the switches to crisis mode. Unthinkable numbers of people lost their lives. The epidemic created panic and uncertainty about our individual and collective futures. We closed borders and quarantined citizens. Economies around the world were hit hard. Hundreds of companies, big and small, went out of business, decimating employment numbers. Most of the businesses that "survived" had to work feverishly to pivot fast to serve their customers' moment-by-moment needs.

Newsfeeds blasted the rapidly evolving situation from every corner of the globe, 24/7. Most of it was terrifying and heartbreaking. The many gaps, flaws, and fragilities in our current systems and organizational structures were revealed. A spectrum of activism grew across the world, reflecting the depths of our fear, frustration, mercy, and hope. We saw a rise of awareness and debate on what is and is not just and how our legal system must address systemic racism. The events highlighted what we've seen throughout history, which is that the law follows what society deems necessary. Along with the unimaginable darkness, we also experienced incredible amounts of creativity and ingenuity from individuals and businesses dedicated to serving humanity's needs.

An Inflection Point

The writing of this book started before the COVID-19 pandemic and was completed somewhere in the middle of its run. Neglecting to acknowledge what humanity is enduring during this time would be naive and irresponsible. We all have been affected by the tremendous influence of the disease.

Every day, we debate the questions of when we might get through the crisis, what it will look like on the other side, and how we can endure until then. Some people talk about when we go back to "normal." Others fear we have lost all certainty and will forevermore be in a daily adjustment mode. Most of us wonder about the viability of those things we hold closest and most dear—entertainment, travel, work, education, and health—fearful of how they may look like on the other side of the pandemic.

But in some (weird) way, this unique time in history has offered us a rare opportunity to assess the mechanics of the operations inside our systems and within the systems of systems. Before COVID, acceleration was the game. Optimizing our business for speed was the priority. We ran internal structures with precision to keep up with the growing demands of meeting ever-stretching financial goals. Growth came in the form of product extensions, updates and mods, and pricing bundles. We pushed harder to get noticed and to sell. Many of us were even optimizing our lives, doing what we needed to do to achieve peak performance, productivity, and personal efficiency. Those max levels were expected for our business and our leadership. Then momentum that had been building over several decades abruptly stopped. The beginning of the pandemic was that very point when many of our businesses learned what it meant to be human-centric.

The pandemic peeled back issues within health-care systems, exposing where things didn't work and problems needed to be solved. It expanded awareness of an already raging mental health crisis. Drug and alcohol use went up. Stress eating, working from home, and limited access to exercise environments caused many people to gain weight, adding to an already concerning health situation. COVID-19 shined a spotlight on the conditions disproportionately affecting vulnerable and marginalized populations: the incarcerated, the homeless, youth in foster care, the elderly in long-term care facilities, individuals earning low incomes, and communities of color. Large numbers of young adults moved back home when they lost their jobs or wages or discovered they could not manage living through a pandemic alone. Working mothers forced to stay home with their children dropped out of the workforce in droves, unable to sustain the simultaneous demands of being mother, wife, and worker. Secondary and tertiary effects of the pandemic will haunt generations to come.

Rising to the challenge of caring for one another in a time of need is fundamentally human-centric. If the pandemic reality didn't render plans, assumptions, forecasts, and growth models irrelevant, it at least put them on indefinite hold. If businesses—and even industries, in some cases—were going to survive, it would take new perspectives and behaviors.

With unimaginable speed, countless numbers of companies closed their doors for good, even as others thrived. Businesses and industries that had grown by creating customer desire through pure marketing efforts could not survive when people's priorities shifted. Companies with organizational cultures built for strong control of inputs and outputs, priorities, and decision-making and focused on delivering products, developing technologies, and outmaneuvering competitors were blindsided by the disruption. Many organizations lacked the infrastructure and tools to switch gears rapidly.

Those companies that had built more flexibility into their culture and operations were able to maneuver to focus on what people needed, rather than on what they had to sell. They tended to find their role in the new marketplace faster and more successfully, in large part because they were demonstrating human-centric behaviors. Whether they provided basic commodity-level demands or connected with deep social and emotional desires, these successful businesses were meeting fundamental human needs.

For decades, most of us have defined and characterized our markets and made projections based on historical beliefs. We honed our perspectives over time, not allowing space to consider disruptive what-ifs for much longer than a passing thought. Vast amounts of energy were dedicated to analyzing and comparing data about our competitors' offerings and pricing strategies against our own. We've used all those efforts to build mental and structural models for how we think our business world works. Allowing ourselves to believe that our customers, competitors, and markets behave consistently gave us a false sense that we could focus on improving our own performance. When everything we believed about behavior got dramatically disrupted, the soft underbellies of many businesses were exposed.

Of course, this scenario oversimplifies the many nuances of why organizations have thrived, survived, or gone under. Rather than assessing issues like cost flow, workforce safety, or financial machinations, it is important to point out that most of the companies that adapted to build resilience have a human-centric element built into their history and plans. The stronger focus on people before COVID-19, the higher their chances of survival during and through the crisis. In a sense, value propositions shifted from what companies wanted to sell to providing what people valued most. This is the heart of human-centric behavior.

Seeing Around the Curve

As we move through the era of COVID-19, speculation is naturally rampant about which adjustments will have a lasting impact and which will be abandoned. We are not lacking for opinions about the top five, ten, thirty, or more things that will be different after COVID-19. Already, businesses are turning to "experts" across multitudes of disciplines to try to get a glimpse into what the future may hold. We're trying to understand and plan for a new normal in every issue and sector from the environment and society to the economy, job markets, and geopolitics. If COVID-19 revealed anything concrete, it's that the future is truly unknowable.

Pundits and thought leaders offer a flood of possibilities. Some embrace the extremes. Others see more incremental evolutions. Depending on what the topic is, one or the other or both may be right. What I would prefer we all do is question and tidy up current beliefs. Does what we do on a daily basis satisfy human-level needs? Do we even know what they are and how our businesses are tied to them? Remember Maslow: people will fulfill their needs for basic subsistence, safety, and security first; love and belonging are a very close second.

We have an opportunity to stand back and assess what happened when the human system came to a grinding halt. As hard as it might be, we need to ask how we acted when that system didn't behave the way we wanted or expected it to.

Food, Fellowship, and Failure

The restaurant business is a financially challenging one during the *best* of times. In a crisis—especially a *health* crisis—it can be exceptionally difficult. The industry is notorious for operating with low profit margins. Owning a successful restaurant takes more than a love of food and community. It requires savvy and precision planning to maintain lean operations and cost controls. The virus has closed a projected twenty thousand businesses. Many will never reopen.

Because restaurants are a place of gathering and connection, people assume that the community will patronize local establishments. And people often do. The restaurant becomes a place where the community goes to enjoy a night out or celebrate a special occasion. (In other words, satisfying Maslowian needs ranging from the most basic sustenance to the higher-level emotional requirements.) What happens to that vision and purpose when people are forced to stay home? What is a gathering spot that feeds the community to do when everyone stays away?

If the restaurant operated using mental models that focused on the tangibles like the place and menu, rather than the needs of people, this shift was deadly. In their time of need, people don't care about business processes, pipelines, supply chain optimization, ambiance, or even artistic notions. They care about getting their basic needs met.

In my neighborhood, the local restaurants that adapted quickly from running a *dining destination* to being a *food source* are largely still in business. They did what Jose Andrés did when he widened his focus from providing culinary experiences to also meeting nutritional needs. He saw what many local restaurants saw: people simply need to eat. That was, of course, easier said than done. The health, environmental, and economic realities of COVID-19 made the task of getting and preparing food much harder for millions of people.

Those restaurants that operated with a focus on people's needs quickly let the community know they were still cooking. They shifted from dine-in to pickup and delivery. They got creative by offering meal kits, take-and-bake options, and grocery items. At the time of this writing, the crisis isn't over for the industry, but we're seeing glimmers of a sustainable operating model for successful restaurants that puts the needs of people first.

Questions abound for those intent on rebuilding the restaurant industry. How will social and behavioral changes adopted during COVID-19 change what people expect from restaurants? What relationships and partnerships developed during the pandemic are still important afterward? How will restaurant owners and managers incorporate possible disruption into their plans and create a more resilient future?

Accelerating the Power Shift

The business media circuit is touting forecasts for the future state of all kinds of industries. When (or will) business travel come back? How will commercial development rebound if everyone is working from home? Will sports welcome huge crowds of live fans again? Is telemedicine here to stay? How will the entertainment industry adjust if audiences decide their home is the new movie theater? The biggest global industries are making adjustments just to survive. Quick predictions offer interesting fodder for conversations, but with so many unknowns and armed only with past growth indicators or industrial measures, predictions are also dangerous.

We had already begun to feel economic power shifts before the pandemic tilted the world. Forward-thinking leaders, such as those who signed the Business Roundtable "Statement on the Purpose of a Corporation," were already putting pressure on corporations to make decisions that transcended shareholder wealth. As it has in many different areas of life, COVID-19 simply accelerated what was already an inevitable change in the balance of power.

We will be sorting through the economic impact data from this historic event for years to come. The forensics of what happened, why it happened, how we could have done better, and what we learned will be the focus for hundreds of academic research papers. People will debate how the COVID-19 economic crisis compared with the Great Depression of the 1930s or the Great Recession of 2007–2009. My belief is that a connective thread in all these studies and debates will be that we gained a greater appreciation for the human system and its impact on business and global governments.

Many aspects of the world and the global economy have changed since the Great Depression, for example, but many important aspects of human behavior remain. There was a general sense of complacency among businesses in the build-up to the stock market crash of 1929. Despite the lessons of history, we saw similar complacency in the few years leading up to the financial market crash of 2008.

Even with empirical information and knowledge, business behavior and decision-making and economic momentum are hard to stop. After the economic crises in the 1930s and late 2000s, financial stewardship emerged to rebuild the economy. As has happened in the past century, we saw an ebb and flow. As the global economy recovers from the 2020 pandemic, it's very possible we will benefit from a refreshed focus on stewardship. Only this time, it will be human-centric. If there has been a global mind shift, it has happened toward human-centric influences.

We already have countless examples of how companies stepped up to support citizens during the crisis. The major telecommunications companies, such as AT&T and Verizon, kept communication up and running. They added work-arounds to increase capacity as more people logged on to work, go to school, and stay entertained while they couldn't leave their homes.

Shopify, an e-commerce platform created to help small businesses with a "business in a box" offering, saw the need to help small and large retailers create sales continuity. A surprising number of large companies lacked an e-commerce site that sold directly to customers because they traditionally had distributed most of their products through third parties. As the pandemic introduced the now ubiquitous concept of social distancing, people changed the way they shopped. Businesses responded by opening e-commerce sites to sell directly to consumers. The 150-year-old Heinz company was one such business. Realizing that many of its customers, including older and more vulnerable groups, were unable to get to physical stores, Heinz quickly created a website to sell directly to those customers who love its products.

Many of these retail businesses chose Shopify. As one industry shifted to combat a financial crisis, another shifted to take advantage of opportunity. Even as larger companies were flocking to Shopify, its leadership kept a focus on the growing number of people who would need to be able to make money from their homes. In an interview with the *Wall Street Journal*, then COO Harley Finkelstein said his company threw out all of its 2020 plans when the pandemic hit. "The entire company simply pivoted as quickly as we could to focus on, 'How do we help small businesses?'"[75] That pivot took the shape of offering a ninety-day free trial for new subscribers and a curbside pickup option that would allow customers to find, buy, and pick up products in the Shopify network. The quick-thinking strategy shift paid off. By the end of Q2 2020, Shopify had almost doubled its $1.58 billion 2019 annual revenue.

Shopify, AT&T, and Verizon are among the countless numbers of companies that adapted quickly to the massive disruption. We saw the flexibility in local restaurants. Big-box stores turned parking lots into drive-in theaters. As we move out of this crisis era, the list of examples is sure to grow.

No doubt, adaptations will have unintended consequences. For example, shutdowns and quarantines during the pandemic drove a significant increase in online shopping. Increased connectivity and broadband capabilities empowered the behavior. While estimates vary, in less than a year, it was projected that online shopping had increased upward of 70 percent.[76]

This massive shift to e-commerce will have impacts on different parts of the system of systems. Most are yet to be determined, such as shipping costs, tax law adjustments, and concerns related to how to dispose of all the increased packaging and shipping materials. Our new shopping behaviors also reshaped spending priorities. Particularly in the midst of the economic hardships brought about by the pandemic, we rethought how we spend money.

Only time will tell what the long-term impact of such shifts will be. Specifically, how will new household spending habits create opportunities to stand back and reconsider the purpose of our business? What obsolete beliefs and behaviors will we need to clean out if we're going to create truly human-centric organizations? And how can our company's actions and influences solve the hard problems affecting humanity?

Leaders will need to fight against the tendency to bounce back like a rubber band into old ways of doing things. A fundamental reorientation in thinking toward human-centric perspectives could make our businesses and governments more effective and resilient, especially in our increasingly hyperconnected world.

Remaking of an Industry?

For me and for many others, travel is a way of life. It changes the way we see the world. The chance to immerse ourselves into different cultures, histories, geographies, and lifestyles can expand our minds and educate in ways formal schooling can't.

My travels have heightened my appreciation and respect for different points of view and ways of living. At times, it's offered a crash course in humility. It has broadened my perspective of humanity and its possibilities. Many of my most cherished memories come from visiting new places. Global aviation has enabled much of who I am and how I see the world. It's why the industry is close to my heart.

COVID-19 brought this beloved infrastructure to its knees.

Aviation is a complicated system of systems. Considering its future offers a challenging and compelling exercise. The human system depends on it, as does our economy. In the United States alone, just moving people through the air contributes approximately $1.8 trillion in economic value—more than 5 percent of the U.S. gross domestic product. It also employs eleven million people.[77]

If that's not enough, moving products by airfreight is a backbone of the global trade system. Every year, trillions of dollars' worth of goods are shipped across the globe by air.[78] Given the speed at which it operates, airfreight is the desired method for shipping both low-volume and high-value shipments. The demands for e-commerce and near real-time delivery that have resulted from the global pandemic will only amplify the pressure on air transport providers to step up.

Here we see one major disruption causing another. The aviation system comprises many intertwined systems such as aircraft manufacturing, airport operations, rental and leasing services, fuel manufacturing (petroleum and biofuels), food catering, and hospitality. It complements and substitutes for other modes of transportation like high-speed rail. Indirectly it induces spending in other areas such as recreation, clothing, and household goods.

It is no wonder that the U.S. government has designated aviation as one of the sixteen categories of critical national infrastructure. The system is so vital to the United States that its incapacitation or destruction would have a debilitating impact on national security, economic stability, and public health and safety.[79] While COVID-19 hasn't destroyed the industry, it has created an unprecedented, almost existential threat to many operators. With air travel dramatically reduced across the planet, this enforced pause has added to the pressure the industry faces to account for its contributions to climate change—reducing the CO_2 emission projections within air transportation has profound implications for global emissions.

Up to the point when a pandemic grounded most passenger flights, the airline industry had to balance maintaining aircraft performance parameters for distance and speed with addressing decarbonization demands. Aircraft and engine manufacturers also have had to simultaneously improve existing products and services while innovating for radical change. For some time, these manufacturers have been investing in electrification and advanced biofuels, but not fast enough, and there is much to do and consider. Technology development is hard and, in many cases, takes time. For example, advancements in alternative jet biofuels and hydrogen must also consider the impact on feedstocks, fuel conversion, and scale-up capabilities.

The confluence of pandemic impacts, ecological expectations, and a sense of global urgency is a lot to expect aviation manufacturers to solve on their own. They're burdened by the strong momentum of past industry behaviors and incentives. And the complex system of systems in which the industry operates demands that other sectors take on some of the responsibilities. Local airport authorities and management, the national airspace and air traffic control systems, regulatory decision-makers, economic development leaders, airline companies, and financial investors all have a role to play in transforming aviation into an ecologically safe, economically productive, human-centric industry.

If COVID-19 has presented any opportunity, it is to "clean sheet" the industry. Identifying important stakeholders and the multitude of interdependencies across the industry is a start. Recognizing the converging forces of old ways of operating, technology opportunities, and rising demands of humanity is next. People will still want to travel to explore. Demand for real-time delivery of goods will increase. More than ever before, air travel will become the preferred method for moving assets for other industries yet to be identified.

Reimagining a world where aviation is able to meet human and market demands, while being environmentally responsible, will take more than new aircraft and propulsion system designs.

It will require rooting out useless or damaging beliefs about how the industry works or needs to work and the incentives that perpetuate the obsoledge. The exercise should go beyond addressing CO_2 emissions to consider other issues within the human system, such as wage discrepancy, diversity and inclusion, and clean water.

Taking a time-out to look at this industry from a human-centric perspective could have potentially immense impacts across the globe. Few places and few people on this planet remain unaffected by aviation. Industry leaders can make a tremendous positive impact on humanity by proactively taking a human-centric perspective to redesign for the future. My hope is they do, because I can't imagine a world where travel is not possible.

A Human-centric Behemoth

A company puts itself at risk when it spends too much time looking inside and not enough time considering the long-term societal impacts going on around it. Having a human-centric perspective is also about looking externally to ask how the organization can innovate to meet the needs of the people who rely on it. We have seen how the flexibility of a small business can allow it to respond quickly, like a community restaurant. But what about the largest company on the planet?

As of 2020, Amazon employs more than six hundred thousand people across a dozen countries. Its platform has more than three million vendors offering more than six hundred million items for sale. The company operates five primary lines of business that serve diverse customers, including individual consumers, other businesses, and even the U.S. government. It is also one of the largest transportation companies, with its massive network of trucks, drones, and airplanes. And its database of human behavior is one of the most comprehensive in the world.[80]

This enormous enterprise cannot be easily analyzed. The company's influence is staggering. Its contributions are wide-reaching. It has clear issues: CEO Jeff Bezos's growing net worth, alleged bad treatment of its workers, anti-union tactics, federal tax avoidance, its global environmental footprint, and the depth and breadth of its reach into our personal lives. Many of these things contribute to its positioning (certainly within the book industry) as an anti-human-centric entity.

But there is another way to look at Amazon—one in which the company has an incredible opportunity to set the bar for what it means to be a human-centric business. If you look at the central purpose of the company, those have been its goals all along.

Before COVID-19, Amazon was an important distribution company. To determine if any of these human-centric values existed, I conducted a limited number of interviews with Amazon employees, asking if the company actively puts people at the forefront. Responses varied in the specific ways that Amazon accomplishes the goal, but directionally, everyone agreed. People reported work flexibility, opportunities to cross-train and advance within the company (with or without a college education), and a company-wide focus on using technology to help people perform better. Many of the employees interviewed also shared that they were proud of the investments the company is making to address environmental issues.

During COVID-19, Amazon's role as critical global infrastructure became abundantly clear, delivering necessary supplies directly to the doorsteps of millions of people who truly needed them to be kept safe, supplied, and resourced (not to mention fed). It prioritized stocking and delivering essential household staples, medical supplies, and other critical products. It temporarily closed nonessential stores in order to divert resources to satisfying the most vital needs with urgency. And it hired more than a hundred thousand more people to help.

As it was growing its global workforce, Amazon also was adjusting more than a hundred operational procedures for the health and safety of employees, including adding rigorous social distancing procedures and regular virus testing. To inform its moves, the company monitored and assessed the changing crisis around the clock. To anticipate possible financial issues and help offset near-term economic hardships for its workforce, the company also raised its minimum wage.

While there were many stories of Amazon facilitating price gouging, behind the scenes, the organization was putting in place the mechanisms to identify, report, and take action against such practices. It removed thousands of offers from stores trying to take advantage of people in need. It worked with state attorney general offices to report criminal or nefarious activities. And it suspended the accounts of those businesses that failed to comply with fair pricing policies.

During COVID, Amazon showed that people were *why* the company existed, and it has served people very well. Regardless of how one feels about Amazon's dominance, its role during the pandemic has been truly human-centric.

But there is much work left for Amazon to do in order to be a leader in human-centric business behavior. As a signatory of the Business Roundtable "Statement on the Purpose of a Corporation," Amazon has the opportunity to lead through action on issues ranging from corporate taxes to solutions for eliminating plastic and cardboard to sustaining community retail to addressing wage inequality. It could take action by investing some of the $35 billion on research and development to create new business models and behaviors that allow for growth without perpetuating the human behavior of mindlessly acquiring items at the click of a button. The investment is important on multiple levels. E-commerce is projected to continue its significant increase, creating the (unintended) consequences of perpetuating the buy-and-dispose mentality that has driven an increase in the use of plastic and paper packaging, which has accelerated humanity's environmental issues. These initiatives must also consider any unintended consequences for the future.

Being a human-centric business means balancing the needs of stakeholders and the business. If the corporate structure becomes unhealthy or ceases to exist, it no longer can serve the needs of customers, suppliers, communities, and those that they employ. For Amazon, this means redefining business from a very different perspective from the past.

Tectonic shifts are happening. COVID-19 showed us that even if we have a prescient sense that a shift is about to happen, we can't predict its impact. Big and small businesses are operating through one of these historical markers. It is an era of volatility and uncertainty. The sheer scale of the disruption—thanks to globalism and technology—is the largest in history.

It's natural to worry. Even armed with incredible amounts of data, most of us are uncertain about the steps to take today to have a secure future. What we all can see, however, is that such a massive disruption also generates unlikely gifts. With our models tested and challenged, better ones emerge. Perhaps we have gotten complacent about paying attention to who our stakeholders actually are. And perhaps there's never been a time like the present to rethink our operating model, remembering that humanity is the only ubiquitous system and the only real source of opportunity for our enterprise.

chapter nine
Creating the Convergence

> The future patterns of global power can only be glimpsed if, instead
> of looking at each major shift of power as an isolated event, we identify
> the common forces running through them.
>
> —Alvin Toffler, *Powershift* (1990)

My friend Jeremy is COO of a large national security company.
He also is a race car driver. A couple of years ago, he and his
wife invited me to join their family to watch the Rolex 24,
also known as the 24 Hours at Daytona. Except for a few drag
races that my uncle had taken me to as a very young child, I
had never been to an endurance racing event, let alone one
that lasts twenty-four hours. It sounded like an interesting
new experience—and a trip to Daytona with great friends in
January is hard to pass up.

In endurance racing, drivers earn primacy on three tracks.
The 24 Hours at Daytona, 12 Hours of Sebring, and the 24
Hours of Le Mans are considered the most challenging and
demanding events. Racers compete to prove who has the
best vehicle and the skills to orchestrate machines, engineers,
strategy, and drivers in flawless harmony during a grueling
battle through changeable conditions.

The Daytona racecourse is approximately 3.5 miles. The
math is astounding. Given that the race is twenty-four hours
long and the cars travel around 135 miles per hour, the drivers
circle the track almost 925 times. By the end of the race, they
have traveled approximately 3,240 miles, more than the
distance from New York City to Los Angeles. It is an incredible

mental and physical feat of strength, endurance, and anticipation. Even though they are following a set course, the racers never really know what lies ahead. Many unexpected challenges can happen throughout the race—most are outside anyone's control.[81]

When competitive race car drivers train, one of the first things they learn is the principle of "look where you want to go." Their ability to travel at high speed requires looking toward where they're headed. It demands focusing attention on their state of mind and on what's happening inside the car, just outside the car, and past the current field of view. In other words, it demands being future focused.

Creating a human-centric organization in today's environment is much like sports car endurance racing. Leaders are the drivers. You're moving fast, around nimble competition, for long periods. You must be consistently focused and relaxed to assess what is working (and what is not) quickly and confidently. Success takes self-awareness, the ability to see the bigger picture, and conditioning. It requires being future focused, thinking about, sensing, and assessing the landscape all the time. It is the practice of continually challenging what you believe is happening, why it is happening, and what could happen next. Agility, wisdom, and intuition are critical to endurance.

To be future focused will require a new set of mental models, not a methodology or how-to instructions—a race plan, not just a great car. The mental models presented throughout this book are tools to help you become future focused to create your human-centric organization. Using these mental models to assess the future helps identify the current and possible impacts of the convergences altering our businesses.

No Crystal Ball

The future is unknowable. You can, however, create a robust future for your organization.

To begin, you must stay diligent in understanding the intricacies of the human system. People and groups of people have their direction and momentum. The human system interacts and influences countless other systems, including our business system, directly and indirectly through other systems. These complex relationships challenge the very reason for our business existence. They most certainly challenge our operating environment.

Being mindful of those things that you cannot control is also a must. The human system is in a perpetual state of change because each person in it evolves continuously. Just as you can't see the future, you can't control this constant state of alteration. What you can do is become more aware of how the world is changing and understand the likely consequences of these changes.

Learning to operate in uncertainty will open a whole new spectrum of possibilities. Optimizing your business around people will bring new and extraordinary capabilities for capitalizing on the uncertainty. Like a race car driver, a human-centric leader must be agile, prepared for the unexpected, humble about his or her abilities and weaknesses, comfortable with the unknown, and constantly sensing the environment.

Of course, as we all know, setting aside time to peer into the future and consider the risks of changes happening to build business resilience is easier said than done. Even if we are committed to these behaviors, many of us feel a constant pull between today's urgent issues and tomorrow's more distant variabilities, which are often strategically more critical to the organization's resilience. It is hard to tune out or fight the momentum of dictates set by our enterprises. Few of us have the discipline or courage sufficient to balance urgent demands and the important work we need to do to create disruption and value in our organization and beyond its boundaries. Those who can do so will be better able to master the complicated and uncertain business environment.

In the turbulence created by the clashing currents of humanity, technology, and residual industrial business models, it is natural to yearn for clear-cut rules, but therein lies the trap. Every day, new advice emerges on bookshelves, in podcasts, in our emails, and on our social media feeds. Management consultants, subject matter experts, investment advisers, economists, and media gurus share their favorite rules and wisdom. Much of the advice is contradictory. We should expect it to be so. Many of those who claim they can help are just like the rest of us: struggling to make sense of what's happening in the world.

These rules are meant to help us choose among many possible courses of action. Yet the opposite is happening. Decision-making is getting harder. It is almost a sure bet that these rules were created with past operating models in mind. So much advice stems from outmoded assumptions. The advanced technology mechanisms and algorithms built to transform data into information reflect yesterday's understanding of how the world works. Further, the algorithms are biased with the limitations of the knowledge of the design team. So how is it possible for them to truly understand the convergences shaping the future? How do we know whom to listen to or what to trust? What do we need to know before choosing a group of new rules to help us with action? Where do we even begin?

Strategic Planning or Something Else

Every year across thousands of success-minded businesses, teams of people become consumed with formal annual strategic planning activities. We gather information, seek consulting support, analyze market data and trends, and review financial data and performance across all business aspects. Teams huddle to peer into the future, attempting to discern where the world will be in a year, two years, or maybe even a few years. Companies try to "game out" their performance assumptions and growth projections using factors like investment scenarios and possible acquisitions. We debate possible competitors' positioning or moves, looking for ways to checkmate them. Dozens of negotiations for resource allocation happen up, down, and across organizational tribes. Thousands of hours go into this urgent work to ensure we maintain direction and momentum in the marketplace.

What makes these massive organizational activities even more onerous is the necessity to align and synchronize our efforts across the enterprise. Most of us are aware of the immense effort our companies put into building, communicating, and measuring our plans. And when we are honest, we have to admit that our execution falls short of our plans more times than not.

Even if we achieve top-line revenue, profit, or EBITA goals, we most likely did so through small, incremental daily adjustments. "Cut this, stop that, or buy those" guidelines become the minute, calculated adjustments we make with our organizational "steering wheel." Those tiny, unceasing decisions keep our race car on the road, pointed forward. Meanwhile, other drivers, looking out ahead, have made investments to create a whole new race car design to revolutionize racing.

Acting as visionaries for our organizations, us leaders share our hopes to outmaneuver disruption. We give speeches in corporate town halls to inspire more from employees to keep our organizations viable and in the game. We fixate on making sure each person in our company understands the complexities of our business environment as defined and redefined by rapid technological change. We talk about risk-taking and seek to enable innovation.

Complacency has no place in this environment. One of the main reasons our teams return to the annual planning table is to combat inertia and its risks. Even with the highest amount of discipline of "opening the aperture" to our thinking about the future, most annual strategic planning activities are an institutionalized process of linking corporate decision-making to budgetary allocations. Most are focused on defining *what* is changing rather than on *why* change might be happening and the disruptions it may produce.

Having supported my share of these activities across a multitude of enterprises, I have reflected on the value of such efforts. I've concluded that, while annual strategic planning efforts focused on budget creation have their place and value, we must make room for deep future-focused thinking. Any strategic planning efforts that neglect future-focused thinking is not actually strategic planning. Rather, it is operational effectiveness planning.

We have been conditioned to believe that most of our annual efforts are strategic, when in reality they are often anything but. Understanding what strategic planning actually *is* requires clarity about what strategy is and how we build it, based on a definition of "winning" the war, not just the day-to-day battles we fight. Winning a battle is a good focus for normal operational planning. Winning the war means you have to continually assess the war you're in, who the adversaries are, what the external influences are, and what winning looks like.

Future-focused thinking is a way of sensing and assessing the landscape all the time. It is the practice of continually challenging what you believe is happening, why it's happening, and what could happen next. It is looking for where things may be converging or diverging. The game theorist and Nobel laureate Thomas Schelling nicely summed up the importance of embracing future-focused thinking: "There is a tendency in our planning to confuse the unfamiliar with the improbable. The contingency we have not considered seriously looks strange; what looks strange is thought improbable; what is improbable need not be considered seriously."[82]

Actually doing future-focused thinking requires that we press pause on regarding immediate risks or other constraints. The process needs to happen outside of today's urgent operational matters so we have the time and space to delve deep into underlying forces and possible alternative futures. This process is not about trying to offset the effect of one future or another. Instead, it's about coming to an understanding that each future state requires a different behavioral adjustment today. Some are better suited than others to do this hard work. These people are more perceptive, open to possibility, and prepared for action.

While we may initiate and guide from the top echelons of our organizations, future-focused thinking is a shared responsibility. It is not achieved by creating a specialized "futures" group responsible for sensing and assessing changing markets. Doing so limits value, because insights are created in isolation from the rest of the organization. Future-focused thinking extends beyond the purview of corporate development, business development, and strategic planning offices, particularly as decision-making is fed by data and extended to the organization's edges. Those at the edge are most likely to recognize when new information becomes important—they're closest to the context of an issue or specific situation. For example, the people who know the most about when to run for their lives from a potential pyroclastic flow are not the Ph.D. volcanologists in charge of an experiment or particular analysis; they're the people who set up the data collection equipment on the edge of the volcano.

Ideally, you should encourage this kind of thinking across the enterprise. You should allow everyone to embrace it, at least to the extent of their proficiency to do so. There are people in your organization who have a natural tendency toward future-focused thinking and mental models. Give them top cover so they have more capacity to challenge and present new thoughts and ideas.

Future-focused thinking is a fundamentally human-centric endeavor. It is a deliberate belief and behavior all at once. It is aware and considerate of the deep fundamentals that are shaping the future. They are core to understanding the convergences creating the future across myriad industries. There are six mental models that comprise these deep fundamentals: time, change, chance, connectivity, constellations, and conflict.[83, 84, 85, 86]

Each mental model is essential to your business decisions. Individually or collectively, they offer filters for thinking about how the future may be evolving and a framework for asking questions about risks and opportunities. Peering at the future using these mental models and a human-centric perspective can give you the clarity and confidence to challenge any of the long-held but obsolete assumptions, biases, and beliefs you need to shed to build resilience and move forward. It is this kind of strategic planning that actually can produce decisions today that are consequential tomorrow.

Time

Time feels like an increasingly limited commodity, as the world continues to accelerate. Disruptions coming at us from known and unexpected sources and angles add pressure and urgency to an already frightening level of velocity. Leaders, teams, and advisers at every level and in corporate boardrooms and business strategy meetings everywhere dedicate fever-ish amounts of effort to developing strategies for speeding up how we operate and scale. Put simply, the stresses of the global environment keep multiplying faster and faster. Some of our organizations are keeping up—but many are not.

Desynchronization is adding to the challenge. Systems, markets, industries, sectors, and cultures all move at different speeds. They progress at various rates of change. The spectrum of these speeds of change is vast inside and across the many systems with which we interact.

We are under pressure to rush within the markets we operate. Technology advancements move at the speed of heat, and business is right behind it, trying to keep up. But our old institutional constructs, beliefs, processes, and policies act as windbreaks, slowing our operations and progress. Our suppliers have their own pace of operations. The educational systems we rely on for a pipeline of well-trained, knowledgeable people tend to change at a remarkably slow rate. And the government agencies and policy makers with which we interact move at the speed of a drugged tortoise.

Across the globe, each culture has its view and philosophy about time and the speed at which things can (or should) get done. Societal shifts seem indiscriminate in the speed of change. Like swirling eddies in the human current, different cultures, groups, perspectives, advocacies, and collective beliefs randomly twist and turn, speed up or slow down.

Most of us do not consider how these varied rhythms affect our businesses. We know they exist. We feel them. They can be a great source of frustration and friction. But they are like sturdy walls that don't budge. Intuitively, we know that pushing harder will not move them. Nonetheless, we continue to push on them, hoping they will start to move at our pace, along-side us.

Perhaps we should study to become horologists, a group of people interested in and knowledgeable about time. Would becoming time experts position us for an advantage? Possibly. Perhaps if we had shared definitions about time's dimension and characteristics in our operating environments, we could normalize the differing rates of change across our business landscape. We would have benchmarks for measuring and tracking changes in speeds and the disruption that desynchronization causes.

Without standards, it's up to you to weigh the context of information and priorities, then decide where, what, and when to accelerate or decelerate for success. Your future-focused thinking must investigate time and differing rates of change. With this insight, you will be better equipped to understand convergences happening and the possible implications.

Change

Even change is changing. We have already shifted from what we once discussed as "normal change" to a state of "revolutionary change." This evolution means that most of the operating models learned during periods of normal change have become not just outmoded; they may have become counterproductive.

During "normal periods," we mostly operated in a sort of equilibrium. In a market economy, supply rises until prices fall, which leads producers to reduce supply. Things return to normal, and stability is restored. In engineering (my first career), this cadence is known as negative feedback. A portion of the output of a system is fed back into the system as an input. It creates a closed-loop process that generates balance by adding just the right amount of correction back into the system.

We have grown up as leaders in a closed-loop business system. Our formal education and experiences have given us a perspective that says that if we do *this*, we can expect *that* to happen. As we have discussed throughout this book, everything—from how we view our business's primary purpose to the organizational structures we have designed to deliver on that purpose to the processes we use to measure effective execution—is geared toward supporting a negative feedback system. A negative feedback loop informs our decision-making processes. How we communicate with customers and build our company's brand have been built on the same premise.

During revolutionary change, the reverse occurs. Positive feedback loops are the norm. These processes multiply outputs. Instead of damping down change, positive feedback loops enhance or amplify them. Self-reinforcing actions tend to move a system *away* from equilibrium, making it more unstable and possibly creating runaway conditions. It doesn't take much to create positive feedback loops. A very small change to a single variable in a system that has been in equilibrium cascades to other variables in a way that stimulates the positive feedback loop.

Future-focused leaders would have spotted the events that led to the creation of e-commerce, therefore creating opportunities to take advantage of it: they would have seen when two immigration lawyers hired a programmer to post their "Green Card Lottery—Final One?" message to as many internet newsgroups as possible, becoming the first internet marketing spam.[87] Add to this the development of graphical user interfaces that made the world wide web usable to the general public. Lastly, they would have brought into their analysis the creation of the PGP encryption system used for both sending emails and sensitive files. They would have watched as it became the de facto standard for email security. These three different events happening in different geographic locations within different professions came together in the same general time frame to radically change the way we purchase goods and services. Sensing the convergence of these events would have allowed future-focused leaders to position and be ready to take advantage of the disruption.

Not all positive feedback loops produce positive results. For example, during the 2016 presidential election cycle, Facebook was publicly challenged for using its platform to disseminate Russian-influenced campaign disinformation and to expose users to political ad targeting. To defend itself against this crisis of transparency and trust, the company hired PR firm Definers Public Affairs to monitor press about the company. Facebook terminated its contract with the firm after the *New York Times* published an article detailing how Facebook hired Definers to counter the criticism about its role in spreading Russian disinformation and its relationship with Cambridge Analytica.[88]

As more publications added their voices to the coverage, more people started to question Facebook's intent and trustworthiness. As more people paid attention to the news and voiced concern, more content on the subject emerged. While the content surely contained factual details, its role in fueling the feedback loop was as subjective as it was objective. People brought their own beliefs and emotions to how they read and responded to the news. It was that public response that did the most damage to the social media giant.

Throughout the crisis period, the company lost a lot of goodwill and trust. At the time of this writing, Facebook is still trying to regain what it lost. And the mistrust that grew and spread during this crisis has spilled over to other companies in the space.

In a time of revolutionary change, the rules of normality cease to apply. Bizarre and unexpected things happen. Unpredictability increases. Long-stable systems become jerky and unbalanced. Trend projections mislead. Surprises, reversals, twists, and turns all play a more significant role than they do during periods of normal change. The growing complexity of the system of systems creates more revolutionary change.

Our businesses are increasingly sensitive to this incredibly disruptive business environment, making shortsightedness particularly dangerous. Coincidentally, this chaotic, changing environment can be an advantage for leaders who incorporate future-focused thinking at all levels in their enterprises. They're more capable of detecting tipping points and addressing them readily. Ask yourself what events you are seeing today and consider how you connect them in your planning. What opportunities or threats are emerging?

Chance

Guy Raz is a human-centric leader. As a journalist, radio host, and cocreator of the NPR program *How I Built This*, he invites leaders of some of our most impressive modern businesses to share their journeys to success. As Raz interviews them, he uncovers their humanness. He exposes their hearts as well as their minds. At the end of each interview, he asks the same question: "When you look back on your journey, how much do you contribute it to skill, hard work, and intelligence, and how much do you contribute to luck?" While he gets many different answers, each interviewee gives at least a tip of a hat to luck, and many offer more than that.

Luck is an ever-present force. In my life, luck opened the door to a job with the U.S. Air Force. It was present when I met Alvin Toffler, which began my consulting career. We often try to categorize times of fortune as good luck and unfortunate events as bad luck. As many of the *How I Built This* interviewees relate, luck teaches humility. We are subject to the unpredictability of chance.

We've reached a point in the Knowledge Age where everyone is connected to everyone and everything. We're hyperconnected to one another. We're tethered to technology. The consequence of these growing numbers of external impacts is that chance has a stronger hand in our future than it used to.

Chaos and complexity theorists like the Nobel Prize–winner Ilya Prigogine have observed that when things become so turbulent that a system is pushed to the point of instability, it is in danger of breaking or collapsing. Even as we gather massive amounts of data to attempt to understand and quell the turbulence, chance exists, making it almost impossible to predict which way things will go. It is no wonder our attempts to control outcomes with a highly regimented direct control of inputs sometimes do not turn out the way we had planned.

Add the considerations of time and change to chance, and we realize that controlling our business environment begins with understanding and accepting the ever-changing new realities. The implications are embedded in individual systems and the interdependent system of systems.

These convergences raise the level of complexity we must manage our way through. It makes the interfaces within and outside our companies hard to coordinate. Decision-making must account for and strive to anticipate the reactions of more numerous and diverse players. It also must consider secondary and tertiary effects of the possible interactions of these players. Technology will help us by giving us insight into reactions, but chance will still play its part. This puts humans at the center of our decision-making. It also raises the value of humans in our organizations. Our human hearts and minds must always be the ultimate deciders.

Connectivity

Over the past few years, it has become more difficult to quantify our connectedness. We began the century with an acceleration into the Knowledge Age. This rapid shift has significantly changed business. The development and distribution of information have become the ultimate productivity and power activities. Global data sharing is ever more essential to our existence. Even the data and technology we thought were obsolete are finding new life in the context of current needs, innovations, and connectivity.

Let's take the example of the flywheel, a technology that has existed for more than eight thousand years. Basically, it is a flat disk attached to a shaft, which is attached to a power source that turns the shaft and causes the wheel to rotate. As it spins, the wheel creates kinetic energy and momentum. The energy keeps the wheel moving and resists changes in rotational speed caused by changes in the shaft's power source.

Thousands of years ago, the flywheel was used to spin a potter's wheel. This seemingly simple innovation allowed for faster production and more uniformity of important pottery. In the late 1700s, the flywheel was used to make steam engines more efficient. In modern times, innovators are using advanced flywheels in various types of power plants to store excess energy that otherwise might be wasted, so that it can be pumped out into the grid when demand is highest.

Hyperconnected networks of people and things create new knowledge at a rate that wildly surpasses any forecasts and predictions. New knowledge is not always born from new inventions. As with the flywheel, it might come from using old technology in new ways or by combining old and new technology in unique combinations to develop something inventive and wonderful. If we look around, it's easy to see hundreds of examples of people connecting and collaborating to produce new knowledge and disruption. Even with the ability to measure the growth and expansion of our global information infrastructure, we struggle to measure how fast knowledge is being created and forgotten or becoming obsolete.

The consensus seems to be that a hyperconnected business ecosystem is the future. The surge in connectivity intertwines people, products, infrastructure, and commerce. There are inherent cost savings, efficiencies, and new revenue streams that we can realize from these interconnected systems. Across markets, we see the unlimited future potential of connectivity, provided we can understand how and where it will grow. The very same information technology that simplifies some of our work also generates new, even greater levels of complexity that, in turn, require more technology to help us manage. This cycle is a perfect positive feedback loop. It also creates opportunities and threats to our existing businesses.

On the one hand, increased connectivity makes us feel like the world is shrinking. Billions of people connect to billions of others. Localized crises fuel global activism. Products made in one part of the world can end up on your doorstep within hours. It takes distance from our list of decision-making calculations.

Connectivity also unleashes massive amounts of information (and misinformation) across our systems of systems. Even with advanced technology, people and organizations have limited ability to filter all the data to make sense of it. Because of the volume of data and the speed with which it grows, it's getting harder to identify what knowledge will be useful in the future, what insight will lose value, and what information we once deemed obsolete will regain merit. In the distant past, data was scarce and valuable. We are now in a time when data is abundant, and our instinct is to save all data collected, to hoard it and savor it. However, only some of it is valuable. In our new existence operating in the Knowledge Age, we must learn how to use what data is relevant in the time frame it is needed and throw the rest of it away.

On the other hand, connectivity also has abstracted the information we share with our customers, employees, suppliers, and the general public. To harness the data deluge, we bundle information into more and more hypothetical classes, categories, generalizations, and models. We communicate with shorter content because we have become reliant on using social media channels and limiting information transfer to just a few characters. The context of information gets truncated, ignored, or lost. Nonetheless, we are making more and more of our business decisions based on information and communication shortcuts. It follows that many of our business conflicts are battles over the credibility or accuracy of information. Connectivity may have brought us closer to people, places, and things, but we are far from using it to solve the enduring problems of business and humanity.

Constellations

Today's advanced information technology is an infinite game. It recombines at incredible speed. The more we use it, the more it is shared. The more it is shared, the more it is adopted by systems. As more technology is adopted by systems, it creates new connections that create other new and diverse systems. These systems of systems of people, business partners, suppliers, sellers, and customers interact across different communication webs (constellations).

Constellations of people and organizational groups form through connection and interactions. They organize for political, social, environmental, or even cultural action. The internet serves as a powerful source for connection and gives a voice to these constellations. They shift and morph depending on the flow of progress, and they grow exponentially in number.

Every one of our businesses is inescapably embedded in a vast, ever-shifting network of systems. Influential business and nonbusiness entities form our constellations of stake-holders. Each constellation has its own rate of change and level of impact on every business's norms, rules, and decisions. They impact our bottom lines, wage decisions, privacy policies, environmental regulations, service lines, and more. And they will have increasing influence as the current of advanced technology gains momentum.

Your future-focused thinking efforts need to take into consideration the ebb and flow of these constellations. They overlap and collide with one another with massive effects on your business. It is crucial to analyze the risk and opportunity of the constellations from a human-centric perspective. Humanity is shifting faster and influencing business in many different ways from in the past. Grassroots activist groups, nongovernmental organizations, hyper-empowered individuals, and new types of trade associations are just some of the examples of human-led influences that will impact how your business is expected to show up. You need to be there with transparency, empathy, understanding, and human-centric action.

No matter how hard you try to control these constellations, they will not be controlled. Nor will they be ignored. Instead, you must do the work to understand them. A future-focused leader will use tools such as social network analysis to identify and understand both overt and covert constellations. Changes within these constellations create opportunities and threats, as do new interactions between different constellations. No longer can we rely on trends in areas like technology, demographics, and product adoption. These perspectives tend to be one-dimensional. For every trend, there is an opposing trend or anti-trend that will challenge your assumptions about where things may be headed. Our mindset needs to resemble that of a 3-D chess master. Strategies, moves, and countermoves happen across three levels. Your business is playing multiple games of 3-D chess across numerous constellations. You must become a master at this new game.

We must collaborate with others inside the constellations we have any interaction with to anticipate, understand, and explore the known and unintentional consequences of our decisions. As interdependencies continue to grow, we must ask "what if?" with every decision and then adapt our internal business behaviors and operations for a connected global society and a changing planet.

Conflict

Conflict is the other side of change—no conflict, no change. Conversely, no change, possibly no conflict. If we are okay with the status quo, we may be able to avoid conflict, at least for a short time. However, our considerations for the future of our business must not ignore the changing nature of the environments we operate in and the conflict happening inside and outside our enterprises that this change creates.

Across the world, enterprise and government leaders strive to create and sustain progress in an increasingly complicated environment. The hyperconnectivity that has driven globalization and collaboration among machines, objects, people, markets, and economies has produced unintended consequences. This very thing that broke down boundaries and pulled societies, economies, businesses, governments, and people into a shared global playing field has continued to evolve, forcing players out. We now face hyper-polar opportunities, struggles for ownership, and demand for shared resources and responsibilities. It has also changed the nature of competition, conflict, and warfare, so much so it can be almost impossible at times to make the distinction between them.

And we must anticipate these new forms of conflict if we are to guide our businesses into the future successfully.

Let's return to the issue of water ownership as an example. In the city of Aleppo, Syria, we have seen the terrifying reality of water being used as a weapon of war. Until 2020, on account of the ongoing civil war, the city was divided between a government-controlled west and rebel-held east. Each side was able to deprive the other of water, creating a state of catastrophe for civilians forced to leave to survive. In communities like Aleppo and others across the globe, the race to control water is a competition that is dangerous for businesses, economies, societies, and, of course, people.

What makes water a particularly high-risk conflict for our businesses is its role in other significant factors. Water shortages are caused by and create climate issues that then lead to agricultural failures and food scarcities. Where farms fail and the environment becomes degraded, migration and urbanization begin to reshape the population. New resources are needed, social norms shift, economic footholds change, and instability flares among individuals, native and new cultures, corporations, and governments. One of our most elemental infrastructures has become a source of worldwide geopolitical conflict that will continue to shape the future for our businesses.

And it doesn't stop with water. As the human population continues to grow, the global supply of usable water diminishes, to the detriment of vegetable and animal food sources. That, in turn, threatens the relationships of countries that live upstream and downstream. The line between competition and warfare, whether cyber, within the supply chain, or in other areas, is blurring. It is becoming hard to distinguish where we are in the competitive environment. The stakes are rising in our decision-making even as uncertainty and chaos ramp up. We must understand what decisions we are about to make that may inadvertently place us somewhere in the spectrum of competition we do not want to be.

Coming Full Circle

A divergence in the balance of technology and humanity threatens our current business ecosystems. Our modern business structures and operating principles are rapidly breaking down and impacting our ability to lead our organizations to successful futures. Even if you don't immediately see it or recognize it as a fact, it doesn't mean it isn't happening. It is. People are asking for real solutions and progress on the critical issues humanity faces. They're demanding you stop the divergence between how and why your business exists. The momentum is growing, and you must give the human system a place of relevance to counter the momentum.

You can find answers by considering how time, change, chance, connectivity, constellations, and conflict affect the currents of humanity, technology, today's archaic organizations, and tomorrow's human-centric businesses. But first you must ask the questions. Give yourself time to step back and look at beliefs, behaviors, and actions currently residing in your organization and within yourself.

A framework for getting started exists. Start with the realization that immense energy exists within the human system. You will find your power source here. Recognize your organization was built for a very different purpose from the one that is needed for the future. Resist the strong momentum to retain the status quo, because choosing not to fight against the force will set a trajectory you cannot sustain through the convergences happening. You will need to disrupt your beliefs and behaviors so you can help lead others into the future. Embrace humility and authenticity, because transparency will be necessary to build trust, and you will need others to trust you if your organization is to succeed.

Understanding the changes outside your organization mandates you make changes inside your organization. Doing so will be an extremely heavy lift. In fact, it might be the hardest thing you do as a professional. You will need courage, honesty, and a lot of self-awareness to consider what's working and what isn't to create the new behaviors and business practices required for the future.

Your choice as a leader is not *whether* to move forward. It is *how*. You can hold on to those tenets, strategies, and practices you've learned and mastered over time. Or you can let them go to make space to adopt new ways of thinking and leading. Progress requires you unlearn old business models and learn new ones for a chance to create a better future for yourself, for the organization you lead, and for the society at large. Those are decisions and behaviors that begin with acknowledging you will face unidentifiable risks and having the courage to embrace the vulnerability it takes to act.

The pathway is not very well defined. There is no map to follow. Naysayers will line up to greet you with doubt and criticism. Some people will hope you fail; some will hope for your success so they can learn, follow, and emulate without having to step out of their safety zone. But like-minded leaders also are trying to find their way to a human-centric perspective. And there are more of them than you may think. Find them, learn from them, share your mistakes and your successes. Take comfort in knowing you are not alone.

The human system is there supporting you. But you must first tap into it.

epilogue

Without some explicit assumptions about the long-range future, and strategic guidelines for dealing with them, without a vision of its own future form, even the largest and seemingly most secure organizations face disaster in a period of revolutionary, technological and economic turbulence.

—Alvin Toffler, *The Adaptive Corporation* (1985)

In August 1973, Kim Dae-jung was a persistent voice for democracy, economic justice, and reconciliation. North Korea's leadership viewed him as a threat. They kidnapped him in Tokyo and arrested and imprisoned him. An assassination attempt and a death sentence threatened his life. Through it all, Kim had vision, tenacity, resilience, and passion for pursuing transformative changes for his country.

During his imprisonment, Kim read Alvin Toffler's *The Third Wave*. He considered the changes sweeping through his country. South Korea had made a historic choice to endeavor to join the ranks of the leading industrialized nations. The country had gone on to pour investment into factory technologies. High-value industrial exports soared, while agricultural and raw material exports fell drastically. The great chaebols arose.

Kim saw beyond the industrial era. As the chaebols grew, the conglomerates diversified their portfolios, investing in manufacturing and technology. Products, innovation, and ingenuity were increasing South Korean exports. Influenced by the Tofflers' writings, he envisioned how South Korea could lead in the coming Information Age. When Kim was released from prison in 1982, he asked to see Toffler before anyone else.

Today, three books are on display inside the Kim Dae-jung Presidential Library and Museum: a Korean Bible, a Korean-English Dictionary, and Toffler's *The Third Wave*. Beneath the last book is the inscription: "He sensed the importance of informanization after reading Elvin [sic] Toffler's *The Third Wave*. This motivated him to lead Korea into an IT power when he became president later."[89] Kim looked beyond the immediacies of what was happening in his world. He challenged accepted wisdom with revolutionary ideas about how the future would unfold.

In February 1998, in the midst of an economic crisis sweeping across Asia, Kim became president of South Korea. He saw the opportunity to use the financial crisis to modernize the South Korean economy. He intended to refocus the country's efforts toward becoming a knowledge-driven economy. Securing a bailout from the International Monetary Fund, Kim developed a future-focused national information and communication technology industry within South Korea. A year later, at the 1999 World Bank Symposium, Kim insightfully told leaders, "In the twenty-first century, intangible elements such as knowledge, information, and cultural creativity will be the source of a nation's competitiveness."

President Kim was a future-focused leader. He understood that the arrival of a revolutionary new form of wealth creation (knowledge) would render the industrial-era economic models obsolete. Under his leadership, South Korea became a world leader in internet and telecommunications. He understood the disruptive implications of the Knowledge Age and urged the maturation of an information infrastructure that would push the country higher on the ladder of progress and also would provide jobs and improve the standard of living for Koreans.

Seeking a global perspective on how to accelerate South Korea into the new economy and sustain its progress for years to come, President Kim engaged Toffler. In June 2001, the two men met at Kim's residence in Seoul for a Blue House ceremony to discuss how South Korea could become a dominant player in the Information Age. Toffler delivered a revolutionary study of South Korea's global leadership challenges and opportunities. The next day, in conjunction with the country's information culture promotion month, he presented a message to hundreds of the nation's business, government, and academic leaders about the main challenges and opportunities that lay ahead for South Korea. It was a call to action for the country to invest in technology for the future and prepare its people for the resulting advancements to come.

South Korea was listed among the leading countries and economies in the 2019 *Global Innovation Index*, copublished by Cornell University, INSEAD, and the World Intellectual Property Organization.[90] By 2020, South Korea had advanced to become the twelfth largest economy globally and was ranked second on Bloomberg's 2020 Innovation Index, having been at the top of the sixty-country list for the previous six years.[91] The country continues to export advanced technology and innovation globally. For example, Samsung is now South Korea's largest chaebol, operating in industries as diverse as electronics, insurance, construction, and shipbuilding.

Future-focused thinking developed South Korea into a global tiger. Kim Dae-jung and Alvin Toffler would be proud.

Back to the Future

What makes a piece of literature a classic? While we can debate the specific criteria, there are a few consistent factors. Classic works tell important stories of universal human concerns.

Although the context or style of writing may become dated over time, the book's message taps into the timelessness of humanity. There is something to learn or be inspired by as you read and reflect on its content and the context it represents. It shifts your views on life. As such, these important works of art are often examined by critics across time spans, attempting to challenge the merits of ideas. But the ideas endure.

The literary works of Alvin and Heidi Toffler are classics.

You may recognize Alvin Toffler's name because you had to read his book *Future Shock* in high school. Or maybe the book sat on a shelf in your family library. You may have been exposed to some of his later publications, such as *The Third Wave, Powershift,* or *War and Anti-War*. Maybe it was a talk show on the television or the radio that you remember. Regardless, I'm almost certain that any exposure to Alvin and Heidi Toffler was somewhere in the latter part of the twentieth century.

If you have never heard of the Tofflers, you may be asking yourself why you should care about people who wrote books and articles about the future decades ago. While some of their works are fifty years old, the ideas, concepts, mental models, and frameworks that support future-focused thinking are as relevant today as they were the day of their initial publication. *What* the Tofflers thought about when they put pen to paper is still interesting. *How* they thought about the convergences happening around them and the possibilities emerging are of the utmost importance to today's leaders.

By revisiting these classic works, you can see how the future came to be and how sometimes seemingly disparate activities converged or diverged to create the world we know today. These are the behaviors we should mimic until future-focused thinking becomes a normal habit.

The Tofflers' way of sensing, thinking, challenging, and questioning is timeless. They used their writings to document the *process* of future-focused thinking. Their writings can still shift our views on life now and into the future, just as they did in previous decades.

Knowing Alvin and Heidi Toffler

It's not an exaggeration to say that the Tofflers were interested in everything. Alvin and Heidi were journalists. They wrote about art, business, culture, technology, congressional activities, current events, welding, and more. They thrived on seeking the truth through investigative interviews and deep research to assemble and verify facts.

The Tofflers were readers whose home was full of books and articles from sources ranging from the *New York Times* to international publications to pop culture magazines. They would read and annotate every day, creating full taxonomies of concepts gleaned from varying sources to build connections and spot a broader meaning that could inform a view of the future.

In 1970, the Tofflers published *Future Shock*. They had spent the previous decade observing and writing about how civilization struggled to recover from World War II. The sixties were a complex crisscross of cultural and political trends. It was a time of turbulence, anger, flamboyance, and revolution, with a counterculture marked by drugs, sexual promiscuity, and rock and roll. Amid this swirl of evolving societal norms and values, the Tofflers detected a far more critical shift. The very pace of change was accelerating. The more they observed, the more they saw evidence of increasing urgency. The pressure to speed up was gaining momentum everywhere, in business, science, technology, medicine, government, finance, and personal daily routines. People were struggling to cope with the profound changes in their lives. The Tofflers warned that "future shock is a time phenomenon, a product of the greatly accelerated rate of change in society. It arises from the superimposition of a new culture on an old one. It is culture shock in one's own society. But its impact is far worse."[92]

Their journalistic tendencies gave the Tofflers the ability to connect with everyone, from presidents of countries, CEOs of global companies, and military commanders to the waitresses, taxi drivers, and hotel clerks they met while traveling the world. Many of these interactions went deep. They were judicious, asking profound questions motivated by a genuine interest in people and their perspectives and understanding of the world around them. Their interest in learning was never fully satisfied.

Their work influenced politicians, generals, executives, musicians, and writers. President Kim was only one of thousands that included former Chinese prime minister Zhao Ziyang, former Soviet leader Mikhail Gorbachev, former House Speaker Newt Gingrich, and some of the most prominent innovators of our time. J. D. Power cites the Tofflers as mentors. Ted Turner credits Alvin Toffler's works with inspiring him to start CNN in 1980. For Steve Case, *The Third Wave* struck like "a lightning bolt" and created his obsession with cyberspace, which ultimately led to his cofounding AOL. And Carlos Slim Helú, one of the world's wealthiest people, admits that much of his fortune has come from his ability to recognize opportunities before anyone else. He attributes that skill to his analysis of Alvin Toffler's works and the deep conversations he had with him. In fact, Slim and Alvin became close friends after they met in the early nineties.

The Tofflers identified meaningful patterns of change and the dependencies between them. In doing so, they uncovered and explained a systematic framework for understanding the clash of forces in today's world. With clarity and optimism, they boldly declared that revolutionary changes would challenge our assumptions about how business, government, and society worked.

They spent a lifetime seeking diverse perspectives, gathering facts, making observations, and communicating to millions. Their confidence in one set of assertions would move them to the next, as they continued to search for understanding. The Tofflers were unmatched in their sustained quest to engage people and ideas. They connected, shared, and extended truth.

Through unwavering dedication, Al and Heidi continued to chart the pace of change. They identified the emergence of the Knowledge Age and characterized the opportunities and issues that humanity would face as societies moved deeper into it. They called everyone to a future consciousness—a commitment to work to understand the future shocks occurring (and yet to occur) and to lead through the disruption for the betterment of all.

They asserted a deep belief in the power of people and promoted a message of hope for the future.

An Unexpected Path

There are always twists and turns in life that take us down unexpected paths. My introduction to Alvin and Heidi Toffler had a profound impact on my professional career. When I discovered their work, they already had eight books in publication, including the bestselling *Future Shock*, *Powershift*, and *The Third Wave*. I am a much different person from who I was before I met them. They influenced the way I see the world, but more important, their influence shaped the way I think and sense what is going on around me and throughout the rest of the world.

My professional journey is unique to me, but the framework is probably pretty similar to yours. Childhood experiences influenced a career choice, and early experiences defined a pathway to follow for professional success. For too long, I held on to comfortable and accepted beliefs and models that prioritized process, tangibility, and status quo over the larger needs of humanity. As such, this book is thirty years in the making.

At a certain point, I decided to take on the challenge of deviating from the familiar, well-trod story line. It was extremely hard and required a lot of trial and error. This book is a business story, a progress story, and a human story. I share my personal story below to highlight a journey. I hope it motivates you to act upon the opportunity to create a healthy and balanced business by making space for future-focused thinking to understand the implications of the convergence of technology and humanity.

Starting at the Beginning

I pursued electrical engineering as a profession, mostly because of my father. He was a master electrician with an innate understanding of how things worked. Growing up, I spent countless hours helping him work on our cars, learning how to fix a bad alternator or replacing worn-out shocks and brake pads. He believed that I should only be allowed to drive a car if I understood that an automobile's function did not rely on the person behind the wheel. The technology and engineering were their own thing, fundamentally agnostic to the human driver.

My parents owned a residential home building company when I was in my junior high and early high school years. They expected that I would help in the construction of new homes. Through this work, I learned how to wire and plumb, roof, and, most important, think through all the detailed design work before breaking ground and starting construction. These influences drove my desire to pursue engineering, which has rules, structure, a correct way to do things, and a wrong way. If you do it right, you can construct something that sustains its form, fit, and function over time and the coming and going of any number of different users.

After graduating with my undergraduate degree, I joined the U.S. Air Force civilian workforce. One of my first assignments was a project that supported an upgrade to the ejection seat within the cockpit of fighter jets. At the time, there were very few women military pilots, but that was changing. The air force needed to retrofit existing fighter jets to accommodate the changing times.

Given differences in height, weight, and bone structure of women and men, it was necessary to redesign the ejection seat for a wider variance of humans. Military aircraft generally stay in the inventory for decades, if not longer. The duration means dozens, possibly hundreds of pilots may fly any one aircraft over its lifetime. The design of the cockpit had to accommodate an unknowable occupant. While the human was important, it was only considered a design variance.

My time with the air force gave me a deep appreciation for how huge and complex organizations operated. It was fascinating to see the intricate processes of hundreds of different offices across the Department of Defense, working together to conceptualize, design, acquire, test, and field some of the most complex systems in the world such as the F-35 Joint Strike Fighter and the Global Positioning System (GPS). It was here that the concept of systems of systems became a foundational framework for my thinking about the dynamics of change and how organizational momentum is a real and powerful phenomenon. I became enthralled with the business of production.

It was time for an MBA.

I took a standard MBA curriculum packed with marketing, accounting, finance, business operations, information technology, and human capital management classes. We read and discussed case studies on common organizational issues and possible courses of action for solutions. We shared our insights about how to manage teams for improved performance. We learned the terms and taxonomies across the language of business. We were quizzed on how policy, processes, and procedures can manage risk and keep a business moving forward and about the decision levers that leaders can use to maximize shareholder return in a competitive market.

In short, the primary focus across the program was learning how to manage an effective and efficient business. We absorbed "real-world" lessons about how to do all these things from our predecessors.

Combining my past experiences as an engineer with my newly minted MBA knowledge, I graduated with confidence that the key to running a successful business was akin to a well-designed machine—sound construction and disciplined operations. I reasoned that humans are important (of course we are), but I also believed that humans create messiness and variables that must be managed within an organization. Only a well-designed organization could accommodate and harness the variables, fluctuations, or unpredictability that may occur because of the nature shifts within the workforce.

In 1997, the Tofflers were hard at work launching a strategy consulting firm. They were activating their passion for helping leaders of public and private organizations create the future rather than react to it. That unique and magnanimous purpose drew me to Toffler Associates. Through a series of serendipitous events, I was tapped to be an original member of the Tofflers' eponymous advisory firm.

My fit with the firm's passion, purpose, and cultural focus was immediate. I was there to help leaders understand the disruptive changes happening around them and to give them the courage and vulnerability to set new courses of action to adapt to a very different future.

I spent twenty years with the firm. During that tenure, I supported hundreds of organizations and the leaders responsible for their success. I also *unlearned* much of what I thought I knew about business success. It wasn't the best organizational design or operational management capability that made a successful business; it was the people.

One particular discussion with a senior leader of one of the world's largest aerospace companies sticks in my mind as an example of how organizations can lose sight of the importance of people. She and I were considering why her line of business was struggling to grow within international markets. Privately, she shared her frustration with the existing workforce: "We just don't hire innovative people anymore. We used to. I just cannot find anyone with new ideas or a willingness to take risks anymore. It is an issue throughout our company."

At this point, I had spent almost ten years supporting her company. I knew the organization and its people. I challenged her observations: "I think you *do* have innovative people, they just can't bring their energy and ideas forward because you and the organization stifle them. Your review process for new ideas is onerous."

Initially, she was stunned, but then she laughed and said, "You know us well. We *do* let a lot of processes drive our behavior."

She recognized what I saw: if you don't embrace human-centric behavior, people will not be able to bring the best of themselves to helping an organization sustain a successful future. And yet processes are a powerful current. Often, they create riptides that you can't swim against. Leaders must learn to swim diagonally to get to the destination of being human-centric.

Future Shock in the Present

The Tofflers' legacy and their impact on thousands of people's thinking, including my own, extend well beyond their books, articles, and speeches. From early in their careers, before their first book, and throughout their lives, they inspired people across the globe to step into the future to consider the present world in its larger context. They challenged conventional thinking and called us all to look deeper at the connections being made across vast topics and issues, encouraging us to understand change and its impact. They wrote books to educate, communicate, and empower individuals to create their future proactively, rather than to be pulled passively into the future. They gave speeches to connect with people, human-to-human; to share ideas and learn; and to champion future-focused consciousness.

I will forever be grateful for the opportunity to have known and worked with Alvin and Heidi Toffler.

As *Convergence* comes to a close, my sincere hope is that I have taken the Tofflers' thinking about the future, humanity, technology, and knowledge into our modern context. Through the stories and entreaties in this book, I hope you've found the capacity and motivation to look more broadly at the future and your place in the changing global ecosystem.

I hope you've uncovered the obsoledge that, when cleared, will free your mind and your organization to innovate in meaningful ways. And I hope that you've embraced a genuinely human-centric future.

That is the future of business, technology, and our shared global society.

gratitude

To Yvonne Merkel: Thank you for conceiving this journey and taking the first steps with me.

To my literary agent, Steven Salpeter at Curtis Brown Ltd., the longtime literary agency for Alvin and Heidi Toffler: Thank you for your persistence in building a bridge from the Tofflers to their legacy.

To my publisher, Chris Heiser, and the entire team at Unnamed Press: Thank you for taking a chance on me. You have given me an opportunity to find my voice.

To J. D. Powers: Thank you for the encouragement to be bolder and take more personal risks.

To Russ Glassman, the Tofflers' longtime friend and board trustee of the Karen Toffler Charitable Trust: Thank you for the support and push to get this book off the ground.

Gratitude to the thousands of clients who offered me the opportunity to work with and get to know them over the past decades: Thank you for allowing me to peer into your organizations and operations and witness your professional struggles and successes. The learning has been humbling and energizing and has provided value beyond measure.

To the many colleagues with whom I have had the honor to work: Thank you for allowing me to learn from you. It has been unforgettable, and I carry each of you in my heart.

Thank you to all who gave their precious time and insights. Through formal interviews and informal chats, you have given me the precious gift of multiple perspectives on convergences happening around us—especially Elizabeth Ross, Dean Amhaus, Dr. Alex Miller, Beth Comstock, Dr. Bryan Alexander, Dr. Paul Nielsen, Aaron Schulman, Dr. Joseph Engelbrecht, Caterina Lasome, Barbara Loftus, Nancy Dolan,

Hazel Henderson, Dr. Dennis Bushell, David Kauffman, Dr. Elizabeth Altman, Dr. Mark Bonchek, Nancy Ham, Dr. Peter Bishop, Lisa Bodell, John Sanei, and Kris Ostergaard.

To Aaron R. Deifel, thank you for all the long walks and runs where you challenged my assumptions. Your perspectives are a source of inspiration.

To my writing coach and mentor, editor, fellow runner, and friend, Rachelle Kuramoto: I have no words to adequately express my gratitude for your time and patience. I literally could not have done this book without you.

To Tom Johnson, an exemplary role model of human-centric leadership: Thank you for the incredible opportunities you have given me. Throughout the twenty years we worked together, you were always steadfast in your support, mentoring, and friendship. I am beyond appreciative for the day you hired me.

I will forever be grateful for the incredibly good fortune to have known Alvin and Heidi Toffler for much of my adult life and to see firsthand the impact of their collaborations and convictions. It was through my interactions with these two incredible people that I learned to see the world differently.

To my parents, George and Roberta Kuspa: Thank you for all the love, encouragement, and early journeys that set in motion a life of adventure and wonderment.

To my son, Gregory, you are the wind beneath my wings.

endnotes

Chapter One: Knowing Humans

[1] Angela Ahrendts, "The Power of Human Energy," filmed at TEDxHollywood, April 2013, Hollywood, CA, TEDx video, 2:19, https://youtu.be/mZNlN31hS78.

[2] A. H. Maslow, "'Higher' and 'Lower' Needs," *Journal of Psychology: Interdisciplinary and Applied* 25, no. 2 (1948): 433–6, https://doi.org/10.1080/00223980.1948.9917386.

[3] Jitendra N. Mishra, "Cross-Cultural Study of Maslow's Need Theory of Motivation," master's thesis, New Jersey Institute of Technology, 1985.

[4] Pamela B. Rutledge, "Social Networks: What Maslow Misses," *Psychology Today* (blog), November 8, 2011, https://www.psychologytoday.com/us/blog/positively-media/201111/social-networks-what-maslow-misses-0.

[5] "Social Media Advertising 101: How to Finally Make It Work for Your Small Business," PaySimple, accessed May 29, 2020, https://paysimple.com/blog/social-media-advertising-101-how-to-finally-make-it-work-for-your-small-business/.

[6] World Economic Forum, *The Future Role of Civil Society*, January 2013, http://www3.weforum.org/docs/WEF_FutureRoleCivilSociety_Report_2013.pdf.

[7] UNESCO Global Education Monitoring Report Team, *Global Education Monitoring Report, 2020: Inclusion and Education: All Means All*, 3rd ed. (Paris: UNESCO, 2020).

[8] "Malala Yousafzai—Nobel Lecture," Nobel Prize, accessed February 27, 2021, https://www.nobelprize.org/prizes/peace/2014/yousafzai/26074-malala-yousafzai-nobel-lecture-2014/.

[9] Luke Henriques-Gomes, "Hundreds of Thousands Attend School Climate Strike Rallies across Australia," *Guardian*, September 20, 2019, https://www.theguardian.com/environment/2019/sep/20/hundreds-of-thousands-attend-school-climate-strike-rallies-across-australia.

[10] Elliott Jaques, *The Changing Culture of a Factory* (New York: Dryden Press, 1952).

[11] Gallup, *State of the Global Workplace* (New York: Gallup Press, 2017), https://www.gallup.com/workplace/238079/state-global-workplace-2017.aspx.

[12] Snežana Lazarević and Jelena Lukić, "Building Smart Organization through Learning and Development of Employees," in *Creative Education for Employment Growth: The Fourth International Conference Employment, Education, and Entrepreneurship*, edited by Radmila Grozdanic and Dragica Jovancevic (Belgrade: Faculty of Business Economics and Entrepreneurship, 2015), 256–68.

Chapter Two: The Human System

[13] Edward N. Lorenz, "Predictability: Does the Flap of a Butterfly's Wings in Brazil Set Off a Tornado in Texas?," lecture, 139th Meeting of the American Association for the Advancement of Science, Boston, MA, December 29, 1972.

[14] Shoshana Zuboff, *The Age of Surveillance Capitalism: The Fight for a Human Future at the New Frontier of Power* (New York: PublicAffairs, 2019).

[15] Shoshana Zuboff, "The Age of Surveillance Capitalism," Institute of Art and Ideas, video, November 18, 2019, https://www.youtube.com/watch?v=8HzW5rzPUy8.

[16] "Antarctic Treaty Consultative Meeting XXXII: Washington Ministerial Declaration on the Fiftieth Anniversary of the Antarctic Treaty," April 6, 2009, https://documents.ats.aq/ATCM32/op/atcm32_op022_e.pdf.

[17] USGS Water Science School, "Ice, Snow, and Glaciers and the Water Cycle," accessed January 29, 2021, https://www.usgs.gov/special-topic/water-science-school/science/ice-snow-and-glaciers-and-water-cycle.

[18] "Our Company," Coca-Cola Company, accessed January 29, 2021, https://www.coca-colacompany.com/company.

[19] Coca-Cola Company, "Improving Our Water Efficiency," August 28, 2018, https://www.coca-colacompany.com/news/improving-our-water-efficiency.

Chapter Three: Recognizing the Chasm

[20] ThinkFoodGroup (website), accessed October 30, 2020, https://thinkfoodgroup.com/.

[21] "José Andrés on *60 Minutes* in 2017: Feeding Puerto Rico," *60 Minutes*, video, 3:01, April 16, 2020, https://www.youtube.com/watch?v=il--ACr5G18.

[22] SEC Report for Tapas Holdings LLC, accessed January 29, 2021, https://sec.report/CIK/0001702058.

[23] ThinkFoodGroup, https://thinkfoodgroup.com/.

[24] Peter Drucker, *The Practice of Management* (New York: Harper & Row, 1954), [page 24] .

[25] Peter Georgescu, *Capitalists, Arise! End Economic Inequality, Grow the Middle Class, Heal the Nation* (Oakland, CA: Berrett-Koehler, 2017).

[26] Frederick Taylor Winslow, *The Principles of Scientific Management* (New York: Harper & Bros., 1915).

[27] Alvin Toffler, *The Adaptive Corporation* (New York: McGraw Hill, 1985), 82.

[28] "McDonald's:-The Story of Lovin' It," Accessed Dec 20,2020, https://www.nextbigbrand.in/mcdonalds-the-story-of-lovin-it/#:~:text=McDonald's%20restaurants%20spread%20across%20120,employing%20more%20than%20210%2C000%20people.

[29] "From the Desk of Jose Andres', Accessed January 1, 2021 https://static1.squarespace.com/static/5b48ae2d96e76ffeb9871ba6/t/5d-

54303663178f0001487b5a/1565798455626/2017+Annual+Report.pdf

[30] Gallup, *State of the Global Workplace*.

[31] "Data Never Sleeps 5.0," infographic, Domo, accessed May 29, 2020, https://web-assets.domo.com/blog/wp-content/uploads/2017/07/17_domo_data-never-sleeps-5-01.png.

[32] Brené Brown, *Braving the Wilderness: The Quest for True Belonging and the Courage to Stand Alone* (New York: Random House, 2017), 78.

Chapter Four: Decision Disruption

[33] Paul Keegan, "Here's What Really Happened at That Company That Set a $70,000 Minimum Wage," *Inc.*, November 2015, https://www.inc.com/magazine/201511/paul-keegan/does-more-pay-mean-more-growth.html.

[34] Robert G. Eccles and Svetlana Klimenko, "The Investor Revolution," *Harvard Business Review*, May–June 2019, 106–16.

[35] FTSE Russell, *Smart Beta: 2018 Global Survey Findings from Asset Owners*, accessed May 29, 2020, https://investmentnews.co.nz/wp-content/uploads/Smartbeta18.pdf.

[36] Laurence D. Fink, interview at the Economic Club of Washington, D.C., April 12, 2017, video, https://www.youtube.com/watch?v=q_j-jRttfV0.

[37] GlobeScan, *From Governance to Purpose to the Fundamental Reshaping of Finance: GlobeScan Analysis: Larry Fink's 2020 CEO Letter and Trends Since 2012*, January 2020, https://globescan.com/wp-content/uploads/2020/01/GlobeScan_Analysis_Larry_Fink_Annual_Letters_to_CEOs_Jan2020.pdf.

[38] Larry Fink, "A Fundamental Reshaping of Finance," BlackRock, January 2020, https://www.blackrock.com/hk/en/larry-fink-ceo-letter.

[39] Chester Barnard, *The Functions of the Executive* (Cambridge, MA: Harvard University Press, 1938).

[40] Tom Monahan, "The Hard Evidence: Business Is Slowing Down," *Fortune*, January 28, 2016, https://fortune.com/2016/01/28/business-decision-making-project-management/.

[41] Arif Cam, Michael Chui, and Bryce Hall, "Global AI Survey: AI Proves Its Worth, but Few Scale Impact," McKinsey & Company, November 22, 2019, https://www.mckinsey.com/featured-insights/artificial-intelligence/global-ai-survey-ai-proves-its-worth-but-few-scale-impact.

[42] LTSE, "The Long-Term Stock Exchange Goes Live," press release, September 9, 2020, https://ltse.com/articles/the-long-term-stock-exchange-goes-live.

[43] Business Roundtable, "Our Commitment," accessed January 29, 2021, https://opportunity.businessroundtable.org/ourcommitment/.

Chapter Five: Overcoming Obsoledge

[44] Greg Roumeliotis and Pamela Barbaglia, "Dealmakers Eye Cross-Border M&A

Recovery as Mega Mergers Roll On," Reuters, December 31, 2019, https://www.reuters.com/article/us-global-deals/dealmakers-eye-cross-border-ma-recovery-as-mega-mergers-roll-on-idUSKBN1YZ0YZ/.

[45] Graham Kenny, "Don't Make This Common M&A Mistake," *Harvard Business Review*, March 16, 2020, https://hbr.org/2020/03/dont-make-this-common-ma-mistake.

[46] Alvin Toffler and Heidi Toffler, *Revolutionary Wealth: How It Will Be Created and How It Will Change Our Lives* (New York: Alfred A. Knopf, 2006).

[47] R. Buckminster Fuller, *Critical Path* (New York: St. Martin's Press, 1982).

[48] Scott Sorokin, "Thriving in a World of 'Knowledge Half-Life,'" *CIO*, April 5, 2019, https://www.cio.com/article/3387637/thriving-in-a-world-of-knowledge-half-life.html.

[49] Ahrendts, "The Power of Human Energy," 10:04.

[50] Toffler and Toffler, *Revolutionary Wealth*.

[51] Toffler and Toffler, *Revolutionary Wealth*, 111.

[52] Colin Forbes, "Transition," *Communication Arts*, November 1992, reprinted in "Colin Forbes on the Structure of Pentagram," Pentagram, March 6, 2018, https://www.pentagram.com/news/colin-forbes-on-the-structure-of-pentagram.

[53] Pavan Arora, "Knowledge Is Obsolete, So Now What?," filmed May 2014 at TEDxFoggyBottom, Washington, D.C., video, 10:09, https://youtu.be/RWR5YX-m2mRg.

[54] Jason Miks and John McIlwaine, "Keeping the World's Children Learning through COVID-19," UNICEF, April 20, 2020, https://www.unicef.org/coronavirus/keeping-worlds-children-learning-through-covid-19.

[55] Riia O'Donnell, "A New Challenge: Recruiting for Jobs That Don't Exist Yet," HR Dive, November 30, 2017, https://www.hrdive.com/news/a-new-challenge-recruiting-for-jobs-that-dont-exist-yet/511592/.

[56] David Gelles, "Hadi Partovi Was Raised in a Revolution. Today He Teaches Kids to Code," *New York Times*, January 17, 2019.

[57] Paul B. Carroll and Chunka Mui, *Billion Dollar Lessons: What You Can Learn from the Most Inexcusable Business Failures of the Last 25 Years* (New York: Portfolio, 2008).

[58] Deb Westphal, "A Clean Sheet Approach to Decision Making," Toffler Associates, July 1, 2014, Tofflerassociates.com (blog post removed).

[59] Mark Bonchek, "How Leaders Can Let Go without Losing Control," *Harvard Business Review*, June 2, 2016, https://hbr.org/2016/06/how-leaders-can-let-go-without-losing-control.

[60] Daniel J. G. Pearce, et al., "Role of Projection in the Control of Bird Flocks," *Proceedings of the National Academy of Sciences of the United States of America* 111, no. 29 (July 7, 2014): 10422–6. https://doi.org/10.1073/pnas.1402202111.

[61] Institute for the Future, *The Next Era of Human/Machine Partnerships*, 2017, www.delltechnologies.com/content/dam/delltechnologies/assets/perspectives/2030/pdf/SR1940_IFTFforDellTechnologies_Human-Machine_070517_readerhigh-res.pdf

[62] "Why Schools Haven't Changed in Hundred of Years," Accessed January 15, 2021 https://www.libertarianism.org/media/free-thoughts/why-schools-havent-changed-hundreds-years

Chapter Six: Leadership Reboot

[63] Eric Coggins, "The History of Leadership Studies and Evolution of Leadership Theories," ToughNickel.com, June 12, 2020, https://toughnickel.com/business/The-History-of-Leadership-Studies-and-Evolution-of-Leadership-Theories.
[64] Brené Brown, *The Gifts of Imperfection: Let Go of Who You Think You are Supposed to be and Embrace Who You Are* (Hazelden Publishing, 2010), [page 26].

Chapter Seven: Truth, Transparency, and Trust

[65] "Was the Media Duped by Elizabeth Holmes?," video, CBS News, May 20, 2018, https://www.cbsnews.com/video/was-the-media-duped-by-elizabeth-holmes/.
[66] U.S. Securities and Exchange Commission, "Theranos, CEO Holmes, and Former President Balwani Charged with Massive Fraud," press release, March 14, 2018, https://www.sec.gov/news/press-release/2018-41.
[67] "2020 Edelman Trust Barometer," Edelman, January 19, 2020, https://www.edelman.com/trustbarometer.
[68] Lee Rainie, Scott Keeter, and Andrew Perrin, "Trust and Distrust in America," Pew Research Center, July 22, 2019, https://www.pewresearch.org/politics/2019/07/22/trust-and-distrust-in-america/.
[69] Sandra J. Sucher and Shalene Gupta, "The Trust Crisis," *Harvard Business Review*, July 16, 2019, https://hbr.org/2019/07/the-trust-crisis.
[70] Jo Craven McGinty, "To Keep Track of World's Data, You'll Need More Than a Yottabyte," *Wall Street Journal*, March 8, 2019.
[71] "McKinsey Digital," Assessed January 15, 2021 https://www.mckinsey.com/business-functions/mckinsey-digital/how-we-help-clients
[72] Sara Spivey, "Why Too Much Data Is a Problem and How to Prevent It," interview by Kimberly A. Whitler, *Forbes*, March 17, 2018, https://www.forbes.com/sites/kimberlywhitler/2018/03/17/why-too-much-data-is-a-problem-and-how-to-prevent-it/.
[73] IBM Institute for Business Value, *Seizing the Data Advantage: Chief Executive Officer Insights from the Global C-Suite Study*, 20th ed., February 2020, https://www.ibm.com/downloads/cas/XAMDQBE7.
[74] Matt Turek, "Artificial Intelligence Colloquium: Media Forensics," video, March 26, 2019, https://www.youtube.com/watch?v=Crfm3vGoBsM.
[75] Jesse Damiani, "A Voice Deepfake Was Used to Scam a CEO out of $243,000," *Forbes*, September 3, 2019, https://www.forbes.com/sites/jesse-

damiani/2019/09/03/a-voice-deepfake-was-used-to-scam-a-ceo-out-of-243000/?sh=59a254d72241.

[76] Richard J. Bernstein, "Thinking on Thought," review of *The Lite of Time Mind*, by Hannah Arendt, *New York Times*, May 28, 1978.

Chapter Eight: Tectonic Shifts

[77] Inti Pacheco, "Shopify, Suddenly Worth $117 Billion, Is One of the Biggest Pandemic Winners," *Wall Street Journal*, September 8, 2020.

[78] "Retail E-commerce Sales Worldwide from 2014 to 2023," Statista, June 2019, https://www.statista.com/statistics/379046/worldwide-retail-e-commerce-sales/.

[79] Federal Aviation Administration, *The Economic Impact of Civil Aviation on the U.S. Economy*, January 2020, https://www.faa.gov/about/plans_reports/media/2020_jan_economic_impact_report.pdf.

[80] "Air Cargo Matters," IATA, accessed January 29, 2021, https://www.iata.org/en/programs/cargo/sustainability/benefits/.

[81] "Presidential Policy Directive—Critical Infrastructure Security and Resilience," PPD-21, February 21, 2013, https://obamawhitehouse.archives.gov/the-press-office/2013/02/12/presidential-policy-directive-critical-infrastructure-security-and-resil.

[82] Amazon.com, Inc., 2019 Annual Report, United States Securities and Exchange Commission Form 10-K, January 30, 2020, https://www.sec.gov/Archives/edgar/data/1018724/000101872420000004/amzn-20191231x10k.htm.

[83] "Research and Development Expenses of Amazon and Microsoft Compared', Accessed January 1, 2021

https://statstic.com/research-and-development-expenses-of-amazon-and-microsoft-compared/

Chapter Nine: Creating the Convergence

[84] Matt Hardigree, "How Cars—and Drivers—Survive the Brutal 24 Hours of Le Mans," *Wired*, June 16, 2017, https://www.wired.com/story/24-hours-le-mans-logistics/.

[85] Thomas C. Schelling, foreword to *Pearl Harbor: Warning and Decision*, by Roberta Wohlstetter (Stanford, CA: Stanford University Press, 1962), vii.

[86] Alvin Toffler and Heidi Toffler, "Beyond Future Shock: Key Concepts of the New Economy, Part 1: The Crucial Difference," *Los Angeles Times* Syndicate, June 2000.

[87] Alvin Toffler and Heidi Toffler, "Beyond Future Shock: Key Concepts of the New Economy, Part 2: How Change Itself Is Changing," *Los Angeles Times* Syndicate, June 2000.

[88] Alvin Toffler and Heidi Toffler, "Beyond Future Shock, Key Concepts of the

New Economy, Part 3: Connections and Constellations," *Los Angeles Times* Syndicate, June 2000

[89] Alvin and Heidi Toffler, "Beyond Future Shock, Key Concepts of the New Economy, Part 4: Concurrence and Conflict," *Los Angeles Times* Syndicate, June 2000.

[90] Finn Brunton, *SPAM: A Shadow History of the Internet* (Cambridge, MA: MIT Press, 2013).

[91] Jack Nicas and Matthew Rosenberg, "A Look Inside the Tactics of Definers, Facebook's Attack Dog," *New York Times*, November 15, 2018.

Epilogue

[92] Donald Kirk, *Korea Betrayed: Kim Dae Jung and Sunshine* (New York: Palgrave Macmillan, 2009).

[93] Soumitra Dutta, Bruno Lanvin, and Sacha Wunsch-Vincent, eds., *Global Innovation Index 2019*, 12th ed. (Geneva: Cornell University, INSEAD, and WIPO, 2019).

[94] Michelle Jamrisko and Wei Lu, "Germany Breaks Korea's Six-Year Streak as Most Innovative Nation," Bloomberg, January 17, 2020, https://www.bloomberg.com/news/articles/2020-01-18/germany-breaks-korea-s-six-year-streak-as-most-innovative-nation.

[95] Alvin Toffler, *Future Shock* (New York: Random House, 1970), [page 92].

bibliography

Ahrendts, Angela. "The Power of Human Energy." Filmed April 2013 at TEDx Hollywood, Hollywood, CA. TEDx video. https://youtu.be/mZNlN31hS78.

"Air Cargo Matters." IATA. Accessed January 29, 2021. https://www.iata.org/en/programs/cargo/sustainability/benefits/.

Altman, Elizabeth J., and Mary Tripsas. "Product to Platform Transitions: Organizational Identity Implications." Working paper 14-045, Harvard Business School, September 10, 2014. https://www.hbs.edu/faculty/Publication%20Files/14-045_fbdbb73e-eaab-40e6-9aae-d874f28d69f8.pdf.

Amazon.com, Inc., 2019 Annual Report. United States Securities and Exchange Commission Form 10-K, January 30, 2020. https://www.sec.gov/Archives/edgar/data/1018724/000101872420000004/amzn-20191231x10k.htm.

"Antarctic Treaty Consultative Meeting XXXII: Washington Ministerial Declaration on the Fiftieth Anniversary of the Antarctic Treaty." April 6, 2009. https://documents.ats.aq/ATCM32/op/atcm32_op022_e.pdf.

Arora, Pavan. "Knowledge Is Obsolete, So Now What?" Filmed May 2014 at TEDx Foggy Bottom, Washington, D.C. TEDx video. https://youtu.be/RWR5Y-Xm2mRg.

Avolio, Bruce, and Fred Luthans. *The High Impact Leader: Moments Matter in Accelerating Authentic Leadership Development*. New York; London: McGraw Hill, 2005.

Bansal, Gagan, et al. "Beyond Accuracy: The Role of Mental Models in Human-AI Team Performance." Association for the Advancement of Artificial Intelligence, 2019. http://crichorvitz.com/gbansal-hcomp19.pdf.

Barnard, Chester. *The Functions of the Executive*. Cambridge, MA: Harvard University Press, 1938.

Beer, Jeff. "Patagonia Founder Yvon Chouinard Talks About the Sustainability Myth, the Problem with Amazon—and Why It's Not Too Late to Save the Planet." *Fast Company*, October 16, 2019. https://www.fastcompany.com/90411397/exclusive-patagonia-founder-yvon-chouinard-talks-about-the-sustainability-myth-the-problem-with-amazon-and-why-its-not-too-late-to-save-the-planet.

Bernstein, Jay Hillel. "Transdisciplinarity: A Review of Its Origins, Development, and Current Issues." *Journal of Research Practice* 11, no. 1 (2015): 1–20. http://jrp.icaap.org/index.php/jrp/article/view/510.

Bernstein, Richard J. "Thinking on Thought." Review of *The Life of Time Mind*, by Hannah Arendt. *New York Times*, May 28, 1978.

Beslik, Sasja. "How Sustainable Is Amazon? An ESG Analysis of the Retail Giant." Medium, May 31, 2020. https://sasjabeslik.medium.com/how-sustainable-is-amazon-an-esg-analysis-of-the-retail-giant-e8b07cc8a8eb.

Bloom, David E. "Population 2020: Demographics Can Be a Potent Driver of the Pace and Process of Economic Development." *Finance & Development*, March 2020, 4–9.

Bonchek, Mark. "How Leaders Can Let Go without Losing Control." *Harvard Business Review*, June 2, 2016. https://hbr.org/2016/06/how-leaders-can-let-go-without-losing-control.

———. "How to Create an Exponential Mindset." *Harvard Business Review*, June 27, 2016. https://hbr.org/2016/07/how-to-create-an-exponential-mindset.

Brenna, Francesco, et al. *Shifting Toward Enterprise-Grade AI: Resolving Data and Skills Gaps to Realize Value*. IBM Institute for Business Value, September 2018. https://www.ibm.com/thought-leadership/institute-business-value/report/enterpriseai.

Brown, Brené. *Braving the Wilderness: The Quest for True Belonging and the Courage to Stand Alone*. New York: Random House, 2017.

———. *Dare to Lead: Brave Work. Tough Conversations. Whole Hearts*. New York: Random House, 2018.

———. *Daring Greatly: How the Courage to Be Vulnerable Transforms the Way We Live, Love, Parent, and Lead*. New York: Avery, 2012.

The Gifts of Imperfection: Let Go of Who You Think You're Supposed to Be and Embrace Who You Are. Hazelden Publishing, 2010

Brunton, Finn. *SPAM: A Shadow History of the Internet*. Cambridge, MA: MIT Press, 2013.

Buchanan, Leigh, and Andrew O'Connell. "A Brief History of Decision Making." *Harvard Business Review*, January 2006. https://hbr.org/2006/01/a-brief-history-of-decision-making.

Bughin, Jacques, et al. "Why Digital Strategies Fail." *McKinsey Quarterly*, January 25, 2018. https://www.mckinsey.com/business-functions/mckinsey-digital/our-insights/why-digital-strategies-fail.

Cagle, Kurt. "The Importance of Context." Medium, May 13, 2017. https://medium.com/@kurtcagle/the-importance-of-context-4ce77ab996c0.

Cam, Arif, Michael Chui, and Bryce Hall. "Global AI Survey: AI Proves Its Worth, but Few Scale Impact." McKinsey & Company, November 22, 2019. https://www.mckinsey.com/featured-insights/artificial-intelligence/global-ai-survey-ai-proves-its-worth-but-few-scale-impact.

Carroll, Paul B., and Chunka Mui. *Billion Dollar Lessons: What You Can Learn from the Most Inexcusable Business Failures of the Last 25 Years*. New York: Portfolio, 2008.

Chatfield, Tom. "Technology in Deep Time: How It Evolves Alongside Us." BBC, February 7, 2019. https://www.bbc.com/future/article/20190207-technology-in-deep-time-how-it-evolves-alongside-us.

Coca-Cola Company. "Improving Our Water Efficiency." August 29, 2018. https://www.coca-colacompany.com/news/improving-our-water-efficiency.

Coggins, Eric. "The History of Leadership Studies and Evolution of Leadership Theories." ToughNickel.com, June 12, 2020. https://toughnickel.com/business/The-History-of-Leadership-Studies-and-Evolution-of-Leadership-Theories.

Cooperrider, Kensy, and Rafael Núñez. "How We Make Sense of Time." *Scientific American*, November 1, 2016. https://www.scientificamerican.com/article/how-we-make-sense-of-time/.

Corporaal, Greetje F., and Vili Lehdonvirta. *Platform Sourcing: How Fortune 500 Firms Are Adopting Online Freelancing Platforms*. Oxford Internet Institute, University of Oxford, 2017. https://www.oii.ox.ac.uk/publications/platform-sourcing.pdf.

Cotsaftis, Ollie. "Human-Centered Design™ Is Bullshit." Medium, May 26, 2019. https://medium.com/this-is-hcd/human-centered-design-is-bullshit-2ff83d-31b5cb.

Damiani, Jesse. "A Voice Deepfake Was Used to Scam a CEO out of $243,000." *Forbes*, September 3, 2019. https://www.forbes.com/sites/jessedamiani/2019/09/03/a-voice-deepfake-was-used-to-scam-a-ceo-out-of-243000/?sh=59a254d72241.

Data, Analytics & AI: How Trust Delivers Value: Findings from the Annual Data & Analytics Global Executive Study. MIT SMR Connections, 2019. https://www.sas.com/en/whitepapers/mit-data-analytics-ai-110173.html.

"Data Never Sleeps 5.0." Infographic. Domo. Accessed May 29, 2020. https://web-assets.domo.com/blog/wp-content/uploads/2017/07/17_domo_data-never-sleeps-5-01.png.

Davenport, Thomas H. "Whatever Happened to Complexity Theory?" *Harvard Business School Publishing*, October 2003.

Drucker, Peter. *The Practice of Management*. New York: Harper & Row, 1954.

Dutta, Soumitra, Bruno Lanvin, and Sacha Wunsch-Vincent, eds. *Global Innovation Index 2019*. 12th ed. Geneva: Cornell University, INSEAD, and WIPO, 2019.

Eccles, Robert G., and Svetlana Klimenko. "The Investor Revolution." *Harvard Business Review*, May–June 2019, 106–16.

Enriquez, Juan. *Right Wrong: How Technology Transforms Our Ethics*. Cambridge, MA: MIT Press, 2020.

Federal Aviation Administration. *The Economic Impact of Civil Aviation on the U.S. Economy*. January 2020. https://www.faa.gov/about/plans_reports/media/2020_jan_economic_impact_report.pdf.

Fiedler, Fred. *A Theory of Leadership Effectiveness*. New York: McGraw Hill, 1967.

Fink, Larry. "A Fundamental Reshaping of Finance." BlackRock, January 2020. https://www.blackrock.com/hk/en/larry-fink-ceo-letter.

Fink, Laurence D. Interview at the Economic Club of Washington, D.C., April 12, 2017. Video. https://www.youtube.com/watch?v=q_j-jRttfV0.

Forbes, Colin. "Transition." *Communication Arts*, November 1992. Reprinted in "Colin Forbes on the Structure of Pentagram." Pentagram, March 6, 2018 https://www.pentagram.com/news/colin-forbes-on-the-structure-of-pentagram.

FTSE Russell. *Smart Beta: 2018 Global Survey Findings from Asset Owners*. Accessed May 29, 2020. https://investmentnews.co.nz/wp-content/uploads/Smartbeta18.pdf.

Fuller, R. Buckminster. *Critical Path*. New York: St. Martin's Press, 1982.

Gallup. *State of the Global Workplace*. New York: Gallup Press, 2017. https://www.gallup.com/workplace/238079/state-global-workplace-2017.aspx.

Gecewicz, Claire, and Lee Rainie. "Why Americans Don't Fully Trust Many Who Hold Positions of Power and Responsibility." Pew Research Center, September 19, 2015. https://www.pewresearch.org/politics/2019/09/19/why-americans-dont-fully-trust-many-who-hold-positions-of-power-and-responsibility/.

Gelles, David. "Hadi Partovi Was Raised in a Revolution. Today He Teaches Kids to Code." *New York Times*, January 17, 2019.

Georgescu, Peter. *Capitalists, Arise! End Economic Inequality, Grow the Middle Class, Heal the Nation.* Oakland, CA: Berrett-Koehler, 2017.

Gleick, James. *Chaos: Making a New Science.* New York: Open Road, 2011.

GlobeScan. *From Good Governance to Purpose and Profit: GlobeScan Analysis of Larry Fink's Annual Letters to CEOs.* January 2019. https://globescan.com/wp-content/uploads/2019/01/GlobeScan_Analysis_BlackRock_Larry_Fink_Annual_Letters_to_CEOs_Jan2019.pdf.

———. *From Governance to Purpose to the Fundamental Reshaping of Finance: GlobeScan Analysis: Larry Fink's 2020 CEO Letter and Trends since 2012.* January 2020. https://globescan.com/wp-content/uploads/2020/01/GlobeScan_Analysis_Larry_Fink_Annual_Letters_to_CEOs_Jan2020.pdf.

Gonfalonieri, Alexandre. "AI & Human-Machine Interface: New Business Models." Towards Data Science, January 5, 2020. https://towardsdatascience.com/ai-human-machine-interface-new-business-models-c0611749c8a5.

Klammer, Adrian, Thomas Grisold, and Stefan Gueldenberg. "Introducing a 'Stop-Doing' Culture: How to Free Your Organization from Rigidity." *Business Horizons* 62, no. 4 (July–August 2019): 451–8.

Handel, Michael I. "Intelligence and the Problem of Strategic Surprise." *Journal of Strategic Studies* 7, no. 3 (1984): 229–81.

Hardigree, Matt. "How Cars—and Drivers—Survive the Brutal 24 Hours of Le Mans." *Wired*, June 16, 2017. https://www.wired.com/story/24-hours-le-mans-logistics/.

Hegarty, Stephanie. "The Boss Who Put Everyone on 70K." BBC News, February 28, 2020. https://www.bbc.com/news/stories-51332811.

Henriques-Gomes, Luke. "Hundreds of Thousands Attend School Climate Strike Rallies across Australia." *Guardian*, September 20, 2019. https://www.theguardian.com/environment/2019/sep/20/hundreds-of-thousands-attend-school-climate-strike-rallies-across-australia.

Herman, Edward S., and Noam Chomsky. *Manufacturing Consent: The Political Economy of the Mass Media.* Updated ed. New York: Pantheon Books, 2002.

IBM Institute for Business Value. *Seizing the Data Advantage: Chief Executive Officer Insights from the Global C-Suite Study*, 20th ed., February 2020. https://www.ibm.com/downloads/cas/XAMDQBE7.

Institute for the Future, *The Next Era of Human/Machine Partnerships*, 2017, www.delltechnologies.com/content/dam/delltechnologies/assets/perspectives/2030/pdf/SR1940_IFTFforDellTechnologies_Human-Machine_070517_readerhigh-res.pdf

Jamrisko, Michelle, and Wei Lu. "Germany Breaks Korea's Six-Year Streak as Most Innovative Nation." Bloomberg, January 17, 2020. https://www.bloomberg.com/news/articles/2020-01-18/germany-breaks-korea-s-six-year-streak-as-most-innovative-nation.

Jaques, Elliott. *The Changing Culture of a Factory.* New York: Dryden Press, 1952.

"José Andrés on *60 Minutes* in 2017: Feeding Puerto Rico." *60 Minutes*, April 16, 2020. Video. https://www.youtube.com/watch?v=il--ACr5G18.

Kahneman, Daniel. *Thinking, Fast and Slow.* New York: Farrar, Straus and Giroux, 2013.

Kavanagh, Jennifer, and Michael D. Rich. *Truth Decay: An Initial Exploration of the Diminishing Role of Facts and Analysis in American Public Life.* Santa Monica, CA: RAND Corporation, 2018.

Keegan, Paul. "Here's What Really Happened at That Company That Set a $70,000 Minimum Wage." *Inc.*, November 2015. https://www.inc.com/magazine/201511/paul-keegan/does-more-pay-mean-more-growth.html.

Kenny, Graham. "Don't Make This Common M&A Mistake." *Harvard Business Review*, March 16, 2020. https://hbr.org/2020/03/dont-make-this-common-ma-mistake.

Kind, Carly. "The Term 'Ethical AI' Is Finally Starting to Mean Something." VentureBeat, August 23, 2020. https://venturebeat.com/2020/08/23/the-term-ethical-ai-is-finally-starting-to-mean-something/.

Kirk, Donald. *Korea Betrayed: Kim Dae Jung and Sunshine.* New York: Palgrave Macmillan, 2009.

Kishan, Saijel. "How Wrong Was Milton Friedman? Harvard Team Quantifies the Ways." Bloomberg, December 1, 2020. https://www.bloomberg.com/news/articles/2020-12-01/how-wrong-was-milton-friedman-harvard-team-quantifies-the-ways.

Kite-Powell, Jennifer. "See How This AI Assistant Helps Recruiters Find the Best Candidates." *Forbes*, August 30, 2018. https://www.forbes.com/sites/jenniferhicks/2018/08/30/see-how-this-ai-assistant-helps-recruiters-find-the-best-candidates/?sh=2e6b5d213765.

Klein, Gary A., et al. *Decision Making in Action: Models & Methods.* Norwood, NJ: Ablex, 1993.

Komarova, Irina, Ekaterina Novikova, and Elena Ustyuzhanina. "Modern Trends of Vertical Integration: Opportunities and Problems." *Information* 20, no. 4 (April 2017): 2373–81.

Kramer, David. "Hydrogen-Powered Aircraft May Be Getting a Lift." *Physics Today*, December 1, 2020, 27.

Lazarević, Snežana, and Jelena Lukić. "Building Smart Organization through Learning and Development of Employees." In *Creative Education for Employment Growth: The Fourth International Conference Employment, Education, and Entrepreneurship*, edited by Radmila Grozdanic and Dragica Jovancevic, 256–68. Belgrade: Faculty of Business Economics and Entrepreneurship, 2015.

Lorenz, Edward N. "Predictability: Does the Flap of a Butterfly's Wings in Brazil

Set Off a Tornado in Texas?" Lecture. 139th Meeting of the American Associa
tion for the Advancement of Science, Boston, MA, December 29, 1972.

LTSE. "The Long-Term Stock Exchange Goes Live." Press release. September 9,
2020. https://ltse.com/articles/the-long-term-stock-exchange-goes-live.

Magzan, Maša. "Mental Models for Leadership Effectiveness: Building Future
Different Than the Past." *Journal of Engineering Management and Competitiveness*
2, no. 2 (2012): 57–63.

"Malala Yousafzai—Nobel Lecture." Nobel Prize. Accessed February 27, 2021.
https://www.nobelprize.org/prizes/peace/2014/yousafzai/26074-malala-
yousafzai-nobel-lecture-2014/.

Manyika, James, et al. *Jobs Lost, Jobs Gained: Workforce Transitions in a Time of
Automation.* McKinsey Global Institute, December 2017. https://www.mck-
insey.com/~/media/McKinsey/Industries/Public%20and%20Social%20
Sector/Our%20Insights/What%20the%20future%20of%20work%20will%20
mean%20for%20jobs%20skills%20and%20wages/

MGI-Jobs-Lost-Jobs-Gained-Executive-summary-December-6-2017.pdf

Maslow, A. H. "'Higher' and 'Lower' Needs." *Journal of Psychology: Interdisciplinary and Applied* 25, no. 2 (1948): 433–6. https://doi.org/10.1080/00223980.194
8.9917386.

Maughan, Tim. "The Modern World Has Finally Become Too Complex for Any of
Us to Understand." OneZero, November 29, 2020. https://onezero.medium.
com/the-modern-world-has-finally-become-too-complex-for-any-of-us-to-un-
derstand-1a0b46fbc292.

"McKinsey Digital," Assessed January 15, 2021
https://www.mckinsey.com/business-functions/mckinsey-digital/how-we-
help-clients

McDonald's Corporation, 2015 Annual Report. United States Securities and
Exchange Commission Form 10-K, February 25, 2016. https://www.sec.gov/
Archives/edgar/data/63908/000006390816000103/mcd-12312015x10k.htm.

McGinty, Jo Craven. "To Keep Track of World's Data, You'll Need More Than a
Yottabyte." *Wall Street Journal,* March 8, 2019.

McGowan, Heather. "Welcome to the Era of Human Capitalism." Nexxworks,
December 19, 2020. https://nexxworks.com/blog/welcome-to-the-era-of-hu-
man-capitalism.

Miks, Jason, and John McIlwaine. "Keeping the World's Children Learning
through COVID-19." UNICEF, April 20, 2020. https://www.unicef.org/coro
navirus/keeping-worlds-children-learning-through-covid-19.

Miranda, Leticia. "With the Spike in Online Shopping Comes a Spike in Con
sumer Data. What Are Retailers Doing with It?" NBC News, December 8, 2020.
https://www.nbcnews.com/business/business-news/spike-online-shopping-
comes-spike-consumer-data-what-are-retailers-n1250349.

Mishra, Jitendra N. "Cross-Cultural Study of Maslow's Need Theory of Motivation." Master's thesis, New Jersey Institute of Technology, 1985.

Mok, Lily, ed. *Future-Proof the IT Workforce: Retrain Your IT Talent for the Future of Business*. Stamford, CT: Gartner, 2019.

Monahan, Tom. "The Hard Evidence: Business Is Slowing Down." *Fortune*, January 28, 2016. https://fortune.com/2016/01/28/business-decision-making-project-management/.

National Academies of Sciences, Engineering, and Medicine. *A Decadal Survey of the Social and Behavioral Sciences: A Research Agenda for Advancing Intelligence Analysis*. Washington, D.C.: National Academies Press, 2019.

Nicas, Jack, and Matthew Rosenberg. "A Look Inside the Tactics of Definers, Facebook's Attack Dog." *New York Times*, November 15, 2018.

Nield, David. "Artificial Intelligence Is Now Smart Enough to Know When It Can't Be Trusted." ScienceAlert, November 25, 2020. https://www.sciencealert.com/neural-networks-are-now-smart-enough-to-know-when-they-shouldn-t-be-trusted.

O'Donnell, Riia. "A New Challenge: Recruiting for Jobs That Don't Exist Yet." HR Dive, November 30, 2017. https://www.hrdive.com/news/a-new-challenge-recruiting-for-jobs-that-dont-exist-yet/511592/.

O'Neil, Cathy. *Weapons of Math Destruction: How Big Data Increases Inequality and Threatens Democracy*. New York: Crown, 2016.

"Our Commitment." Business Roundtable. Accessed January 29, 2021. https://opportunity.businessroundtable.org/ourcommitment/.

"Our Company." Coca-Cola Company. Accessed January 29, 2021. https://www.coca-colacompany.com/company.

Pacheco, Inti. "Shopify, Suddenly Worth $117 Billion, Is One of the Biggest Pandemic Winners." *Wall Street Journal*, September 8, 2020

Pappano, Laura. "Is the College Degree Outdated?" *Hechinger Report*, April 27, 2017. https://hechingerreport.org/college-degree-outdated/.

Pearce, Daniel J. G., et al. "Role of Projection in the Control of Bird Flocks." *Proceedings of the National Academy of Sciences of the United States of America* 111, no. 29 (July 7, 2014): 10422–6. https://doi.org/10.1073/pnas.1402202111.

Pearlstein, Steven. "When Shareholder Capitalism Came to Town." *American Prospect*, April 19, 2014. https://prospect.org/economy/shareholder-capitalism-came-town/.

"Presidential Policy Directive—Critical Infrastructure Security and Resilience." PPD-21. February 21, 2013. https://obamawhitehouse.archives.gov/the-press-office/2013/02/12/presidential-policy-directive-critical-infrastructure-security-and-resil.

Prigogine, Ilya, and Isabelle Stengers. *Order Out of Chaos: Man's New Dialogue with Nature*. New York: Bantam, 1984.

Pritchard, Duncan, John Turri, and J. Adam Carter. "The Value of Knowledge." In *Stanford Encyclopedia of Philosophy*, edited by Edward N. Zalta. Spring 2018 ed. https://plato.stanford.edu/entries/knowledge-value/.

Rahim, Zamira. "Algorithms Can Drive Inequality. Just Look at Britain's School

Exam Chaos." CNN, August 23, 2020. https://www.cnn.com/2020/08/23/tech/algorithms-bias-inequality-intl-gbr/index.html.

Rainie, Lee, and Janna Anderson. "Code-Dependent: Pros and Cons of the Algorithm Age." Pew Research Center, February 8, 2017. https://www.pewresearch.org/internet/2017/02/08/code-dependent-pros-and-cons-of-the-algorithm-age/.

Rainie, Lee, Scott Keeter, and Andrew Perrin. "Trust and Distrust in America." Pew Research Center, July 22, 2019. https://www.pewresearch.org/politics/2019/07/22/trust-and-distrust-in-america/.

"Research and Development Expenses of Amazon and Microsoft Compared', Accessed January 1, 2021, https://statstic.com/research-and-development-expenses-of-amazon-and-microsoft-compared/

"Retail E-commerce Sales Worldwide from 2014 to 2023." Statista, June 2019. https://www.statista.com/statistics/379046/worldwide-retail-e-commerce-sales/.

Roumeliotis, Greg, and Pamela Barbaglia. "Dealmakers Eye Cross-Border M&A Recovery as Mega Mergers Roll On." Reuters, December 31, 2019. https://www.reuters.com/article/us-global-deals/dealmakers-eye-cross-border-ma-recovery-as-mega-mergers-roll-on-idUSKBN1YZ0YZ/.

Rutledge, Pamela B. "Social Networks: What Maslow Misses." *Psychology Today* (blog), November 8, 2011. https://www.psychologytoday.com/us/blog/positively-media/201111/social-networks-what-maslow-misses-0.

Schelling, Thomas C. Foreword to *Pearl Harbor: Warning and Decision*, by Roberta Wohlstetter. Stanford, CA: Stanford University Press, 1962.

Schilling, David Russell. "Knowledge Doubling Every 12 Months, Soon to Be Every 12 Hours." Industry Tap, April 19, 2013. https://www.industrytap.com/knowledge-doubling-every-12-months-soon-to-be-every-12-hours/3950.

SEC Report for Tapas Holdings LLC. Accessed January 29, 2021. https://sec.report/CIK/0001702058.

Senge, Peter. *The Fifth Discipline: The Art and Practice of the Learning Organization*. New York: Doubleday, 1990.

Silberg, Jake, and James Manyika. "Notes from the AI Frontier: Tackling Bias in AI (and in Humans)." McKinsey Global Institute, June 2019. https://www.mckinsey.com/~/media/mckinsey/featured%20insights/artificial%20intelligence/tackling%20bias%20in%20artificial%20intelligence%20and%20in%20humans/mgi-tackling-bias-in-ai-june-2019.pdf.

Singer, P. W., and Emerson T. Brooking. *LikeWar: The Weaponization of Social Media*. New York: Houghton Mifflin Harcourt, 2019.

"Social Media Advertising 101: How to Finally Make It Work for Your Small Business." PaySimple, accessed May 29, 2020. https://paysimple.com/blog/social-media-advertising-101-how-to-finally-make-it-work-for-your-small-business/.

Sorokin, Scott. "Thriving in a World of 'Knowledge Half-Life.'" *CIO*, April 5, 2019.

https://www.cio.com/article/3387637/thriving-in-a-world-of-knowledge-half-life.html.

Spivey, Sara. "Why Too Much Data Is a Problem and How to Prevent It." Inter view by Kimberly A. Whitler. *Forbes*, March 17, 2018. https://www.forbes.com/sites/kimberlywhitler/2018/03/17/why-too-much-data-is-a-problem-and-how-to-prevent-it/.

Stephens-Davidowitz, Seth. *Everybody Lies: Big Data, New Data, and What the Internet Can Tell Us About Who We Really Are*. New York: Dey Street, 2017.

Stoll, John D. "Sustainability Was Corporate America's Buzzword. This Crisis Changes That." *Wall Street Journal*, May 1, 2020.

Strong, Colin. "Big Data Doesn't Speak For Itself." Video. March 23, 2015. https://www.youtube.com/watch?v=h_hFTdSyf_k&t=58s.

Sucher, Sandra J., and Shalene Gupta. "The Trust Crisis." *Harvard Business Review*, July 16, 2019. https://hbr.org/2019/07/the-trust-crisis.

Swisher, Kara. "Amazon Wants to Get Even Closer. Skintight." *New York Times*, November 27, 2020.

ThinkFoodGroup (website). Accessed October 30, 2020. https://thinkfoodgroup.com/.

Toews, Rob. "Deepfakes Are Going to Wreak Havoc on Society. We Are Not Prepared." *Forbes*, May 25, 2020.

Toffler, Alvin. *The Adaptive Corporation*. New York: McGraw Hill, 1985.

Toffler, Alvin, and Heidi Toffler. "Beyond Future Shock: After the Digital Revolution: The Fourth Wave Arrives." *Los Angeles Times* Syndicate, October 1999.

———. "Beyond Future Shock: Key Concepts of the New Economy, Part 1: The Crucial Difference." *Los Angeles Times* Syndicate, June 2000.

———. "Beyond Future Shock: Key Concepts of the New Economy, Part 2: How Change Itself Is Changing." *Los Angeles Times* Syndicate, June 2000.

———. "Beyond Future Shock: Key Concepts of the New Economy, Part 3: Connections and Constellations." *Los Angeles Times* Syndicate, June 2000.

———. "Beyond Future Shock: Key Concepts of the New Economy, Part 4: Con currence and Conflict." *Los Angeles Times* Syndicate, June 2000.

———. *Revolutionary Wealth: How It Will Be Created and How It Will Change Our Lives*. New York: Alfred A. Knopf, 2006.

Turek, Matt. "Artificial Intelligence Colloquium: Media Forensics." Video. March 26, 2019. https://www.youtube.com/watch?v=Crfm3vGoBsM.

Turner, Darren. "How to Become an Endurance Driver." Interview by Joe Holding. Top Gear, April 15, 2016. https://www.topgear.com/car-news/british/how-be-come-endurance-driver#1.

"2020 Edelman Trust Barometer." Edelman, January 19, 2020. https://www.edelman.com/trustbarometer.

UNESCO Global Education Monitoring Report Team. *Global Education Monitoring Report, 2020: Inclusion and Education: All Means All*. 3rd ed. Paris: UNESCO, 2020.

USGS Water Science School. "Ice, Snow, and Glaciers and the Water Cycle." Accessed January 29, 2021. https://www.usgs.gov/special-topic/water-sci

ence-school/science/ice-snow-and-glaciers-and-water-cycle.

U.S. Securities and Exchange Commission. "Theranos, CEO Holmes, and Former President Balwani Charged with Massive Fraud." Press release, March 14, 2018. https://www.sec.gov/news/press-release/2018-41.

Walsh, Mike. "Why Business Leaders Need to Understand Their Algorithms." *Harvard Business Review*, November 19, 2019. https://hbr.org/2019/11/why-business-leaders-need-to-understand-their-algorithms.

"Was the Media Duped by Elizabeth Holmes?" CBS News, May 20, 2018. Video. https://www.cbsnews.com/video/was-the-media-duped-by-elizabeth-holmes/.

Westphal, Deb. "A Clean Sheet Approach to Decision Making." Toffler Associates, July 1, 2014. tofflerassociates.com (blog post removed).

"Why Schools Haven't Changed in Hundred of Years," Accessed January 15, 2021 https://www.libertarianism.org/media/free-thoughts/why-schools-havent-changed-hundreds-years

Whyte, William Foote. "Social Inventions for Solving Human Problems." *Clinical Sociology Review* 5, no. 1 (1987). https://digitalcommons.wayne.edu/csr/vol5/iss1/7.

Wittlief, Matt. "How to Get Business Leaders to Trust Algorithms." *BizTech*, June 20, 2018. https://biztechmagazine.com/article/2018/06/how-get-business-leaders-trust-algorithms.

Winslow, Frederick Taylor. *The Principles of Scientific Management*. New York: Harper & Bros., 1915.

World Economic Forum. *The Future Role of Civil Society*. January 2013. http://www3.weforum.org/docs/WEF_FutureRoleCivilSociety_Report_2013.pdf.

———. *The Global Risks Report 2020*. January 2020. https://www.weforum.org/reports/the-global-risks-report-2020.

Zuboff, Shoshana. "The Age of Surveillance Capitalism." Institute of Art and Ideas, November 18, 2019. Video. https://www.youtube.com/watch?v=8HzW5rzPUy8.

———. *The Age of Surveillance Capitalism: The Fight for a Human Future at the New Frontier of Power*. New York: PublicAffairs, 2019.

about the author

Deborah Westphal is a passionate humanist who has guided our era's top minds and leaders to challenge biases, ignite ideas, and build connections and resilience for a secure and sound future. Her career spans more than thirty years in government agencies and Fortune 100 companies and on virtually every continent. In 1999, Alvin Toffler tapped her as one of the founding members of his eponymous consulting firm, Toffler Associates. From 2007 through 2018, she served as the firm's CEO and has since contributed her experience and knowledge as a member of the board. Through her work, she has guided notable organizations including Lockheed Martin, Northrop Grumman, Marriott, the U.S. Air Force, Baxter International, Bayer, Heinz, Microsoft, Koppers, PPG, DARPA, the National Security Agency, Loral Space & Communications, NASA, Qwest, Verizon, and Westinghouse.

Deborah's empathetic and thought-provoking style helps readers spot patterns that signify future risks and opportunities. She's a sought-after speaker and writer who provided the foreword to the essay collection *After Shock*.

Deborah is a world traveler who enjoys time with her son and running in the mountains.